The German Shepherd

Our Best Friends

The Boxer
Caring for Your Mutt
The German Shepherd
The Golden Retriever
The Labrador Retriever
The Poodle
The Shih Tzu
The Yorkshire Terrier

OUR BEST FRIENDS

The German Shepherd

September Morn

ELDORADO INK

Produced by OTTN Publishing, Stockton, New Jersey

Eldorado Ink
PO Box 100097
Pittsburgh, PA 15233
www.eldoradoink.com

First printing

1 3 5 7 9 8 6 4 2

Library of Congress Cataloging-in-Publication Data

Morn, September B.
  The German shepherd / September Morn.
     p. cm. — (Our best friends)
  Includes bibliographical references and index.
  ISBN-13: 978-1-932904-21-5 (hc)
  ISBN-10: 1-932904-21-2 (hc)
  1. German shepherd dog. I. Title.
  SF429.G37M68 2008
  636.737'6—dc22

                                    2007044875

Photo credits: © American Animal Hospital Association: 41; Courtesy American Kennel Club,
www.akc.org: 22; Hulton Archive/Getty Images: 19, 21; © iStockphoto.com/Mark Baskett: 96;
© iStockphoto.com/Tuomas Elenius: 81; © iStockphoto.com/FrankMarkSerge: 54; © iStockphoto.com/
Gina Hanf: 29; © iStockphoto.com/Geoff Hardy: 93; © iStockphoto.com/Radoslaw Kostka: 85;
© iStockphoto.com/Jason Lugo: 12 (right); © iStockphoto.com/Bryan Malley: 55; © iStockphoto.com/
Gary Martin: 45; © iStockphoto.com/Kati Neudert: 40, 44, 51, 86; © iStockphoto.com/
niknikon: 97; © iStockphoto.com/Iztok Noc: 94; © iStockphoto.com/Guillermo Perales: 48;
© iStockphoto.com/Kevin Russ: 3, front cover (left center); © iStockphoto.com/Craig Smith: 75;
© iStockphoto.com/Sergii Sokurenko: 37; © iStockphoto.com/Nikolai Tsvetkov: 70; © Joel Mills, 77;
Courtesy National Association of Professional Pet Sitters, www.petsitters.org: 73; © Will Patch: 53; used
under license from Shutterstock, Inc.: 8, 10, 11, 12 (left), 13, 14, 16, 18 (flag and dogs), 23, 24, 25, 26,
27, 28, 31, 32, 34, 35, 39, 42, 43, 46, 49, 52, 57, 59, 60, 61, 62, 65 (all), 67, 68, 69, 71, 74, 78, 79, 82,
83, 87, 89, 98, 99, 100, front cover (main, left top, and left bottom), back cover.

TABLE OF CONTENTS

Introduction by Gary Korsgaard, DVM		**6**
1	**Is a German Shepherd Right for You?**	**9**
2	**Breed History and Background**	**18**
3	**Responsible Pet Ownership**	**26**
4	**The Best Possible Beginning**	**34**
5	**Caring for Your Shepherd Puppy (Birth to Six Months)**	**43**
6	**Things to Know as Your Shepherd Grows**	**62**
7	**Caring for Your Adult Dog**	**74**
8	**Caring for Your Senior Dog**	**96**
	Organizations to Contact	**102**
	Further Reading	**105**
	Internet Resources	**106**
	Index	**108**
	About the Author	**112**

Introduction

GARY KORSGAARD, DVM

The mutually beneficial relationship between humans and animals began long before the dawn of recorded history. Archaeologists believe that humans began to capture and tame wild goats, sheep, and pigs more than 9,000 years ago. These animals were then bred for specific purposes, such as providing humans with a reliable source of food or providing furs and hides that could be used for clothing or the construction of dwellings.

Other animals had been sought for companionship and assistance even earlier. The dog, believed to be the first animal domesticated, began living and working with Stone Age humans in Europe more than 14,000 years ago. Some archaeologists believe that wild dogs and humans were drawn together because both hunted the same prey. By taming and training dogs, humans became more effective hunters. Dogs, meanwhile, enjoyed the social contact with humans and benefited from greater access to food and warm shelter. Dogs soon became beloved pets as well as trusted workers. This can be seen from the many artifacts depicting dogs that have been found at ancient sites in Asia, Europe, North America, and the Middle East.

The earliest domestic cats appeared in the Middle East about 5,000 years ago. Small wild cats were probably first attracted to human settlements because plenty of rodents could be found wherever harvested grain was stored. Cats played a useful role in hunting and killing these pests, and it is likely that grateful humans rewarded them for this assistance. Over time, these small cats gave up some of their aggressive wild behaviors and began living among humans. Cats eventually became so popular in ancient Egypt that they were believed to possess magical powers. Cat statues were placed outside homes to ward off evil spirits, and mummified cats were included in royal tombs to accompany their owners into the afterlife.

Today, few people believe that cats have supernatural powers, but most pet owners feel a magical bond with their pets, whether they are dogs, cats, hamsters, rabbits, horses, or parrots. The lives of pets and their people become inextricably intertwined, providing strong emotional and physical rewards for both humans and animals. People of all ages can benefit from the loving companionship of a pet. Not surprisingly, then, pet ownership is widespread. Recent statistics indicate that about 60 percent of all households in the United States and Canada have at least one pet, while the figure is close to 50 percent of households in the United Kingdom. For millions of people, therefore, pets truly have become their "best friends."

Finding the best animal friend can be a challenge, however. Not only are there many types of domesticated pets, but each has specific needs, characteristics, and personality traits. Even within a category of pets, such as dogs, different breeds will flourish in different surroundings and with different treatment. For example, a German Shepherd may not be the right pet for a person living in a cramped urban apartment; that person might be better off caring for a smaller dog like a Toy Poodle or Shih Tzu, or perhaps a cat. On the other hand, an active person who loves the outdoors may prefer the companionship of a Labrador Retriever to that of a small dog or a passive indoor pet like a goldfish or hamster.

The joys of pet ownership come with certain responsibilities. Bringing a pet into your home and your neighborhood obligates you to care for and train the pet properly. For example, a dog must be housebroken, taught to obey your commands, and trained to behave appropriately when he encounters other people or animals. Owners must also be mindful of their pet's particular nutritional and medical needs.

The purpose of the OUR BEST FRIENDS series is to provide a helpful and comprehensive introduction to pet ownership. Each book contains the basic information a prospective pet owner needs in order to choose the right pet for his or her situation and to care for that pet throughout the pet's lifetime. Training, socialization, proper nutrition, potential medical issues, and the legal responsibilities of pet ownership are thoroughly explained and discussed, and an abundance of expert tips and suggestions are offered. Whether it is a hamster, corn snake, guinea pig, or Labrador Retriever, the books in the OUR BEST FRIENDS series provide everything the reader needs to know about how to have a happy, well-adjusted, and well-behaved pet.

The intelligent and protective nature of the German Shepherd breed makes them excellent pets as well as outstanding service dogs.

CHAPTER ONE

Is a German Shepherd Right for You?

The German Shepherd is a marvel of strength and agility, courage and dignity, loyalty and obedience. German Shepherds are versatile dogs, capable of performing a wide variety of tasks extremely well. Shepherds learn quickly and have excellent retention. They make wonderful family dogs and personal companions because they are absolutely devoted to their people. It is not surprising that these nobly handsome and extremely intelligent dogs are popular animal companions all around the world.

German Shepherds are bred to work, and enjoy performing tasks and tricks that make them feel useful and appreciated. Shepherds will enthusiastically carry out whatever jobs they are trained to do. Even small jobs, like fetching his own leash before walks, will evoke in a German Shepherd the sense of duty and pride that defines this exceptional breed.

A German Shepherd not assigned a task to keep him busy and satisfied will usually make up some duties on his own. A shepherd will typically adopt the role of sentry and guard of the home property. Shepherds living with families often become vigilant protectors of the children. Many shepherds act bossy around fellow pets and other animals, taking it upon themselves to keep all cats off the dining room table or shoo away chickens that peck too close to the garden.

Left to their own devices, shepherds can get carried away with their self-appointed duties. This can result in behavior problems that require intensive retraining of the dog. For example, the shepherd that assumes responsibility for a family's children may decide one day to refuse entry to the children's friends. Some self-appointed dog jobs are unacceptable from the beginning—like guarding the homes on either side from the neighbors who live there. Those types of bored-shepherd jobs will quickly lose friends for the dogs' owners and may incur some embarrassing and expensive visits from animal control.

The full-grown German Shepherd has a regal, majestic appearance.

To live happily with a German Shepherd, you need to train him and guide him to behave the way you want. You also need to provide him with daily physical and mental exercise. If your lifestyle keeps you away from home for long workdays all week, and then on weekends you enjoy activities that don't involve dogs, you may not realistically be able to provide the level of physical exercise and mental stimulation that will keep a German Shepherd healthy and happy. However, if you relish the steady, devoted companionship of a loyal, intelligent, strong, handsome, large dog, and are willing and able to provide sufficient daily exercise and mental stimulation for such a dog, a German Shepherd may be an ideal choice.

If you enjoy training and interacting with a very smart dog and you value a canine pal who applies himself wholeheartedly to any duty or job you teach him, then a German Shepherd could be your perfect match. If you already have a job in mind for your dog—whether as a working farm dog, a show-ring competitor, a full-time buddy, a search-and-rescue partner, a pet-therapy dog, or a watchful home protector—a German Shepherd can do the job and do it well.

APPEARANCE AND CHARACTERISTICS OF THE BREED

German Shepherds are large and rugged, yet elegant and graceful, standing from 22 to 26 inches (56 to 66 cm) tall at the shoulder. They have erect ears; dark, almond-shaped eyes; and a fairly long, wedge-shaped muzzle. The dignified, direct, and fearless expression of the German Shepherd is sometimes described as the "look of eagles."

When a German Shepherd walks, there is purpose and strength to his stride but also a lightness in his step that is surprising in a dog this large and heavy. At a gallop, the shepherd's long, graceful, bounding strides can easily keep up with a cantering horse. But it is the German Shepherd's trot that is the hallmark gait of this breed. Most dogs, when moving at a trot, maintain ground contact with two of their paws at each step. The German Shepherd, however, has a very fast suspended trot, where for a moment of each stride, all four paws are off the

A German Shepherd leaps into a lake, displaying his long, lean body.

ground. This gives the shepherd's trot the appearance that the dog is flying or floating, especially when viewed from the side.

The German Shepherd has a medium-length double coat, with stiff, weather-repelling outer guard hairs, and soft, fluffy, insulating undercoat fur. In winter, the undercoat grows thicker and denser to provide extra insulation and protection from harsh weather. The summer coat comprises mostly guard hairs, with almost no

underfur, and this thinner coat allows the dog's body to cool itself more efficiently during hot weather.

When the shepherd undergoes its twice-a-year seasonal shedding, these dogs drop huge amounts of undercoat and guard hairs. During this period they need brushing or combing every day. (The owner's house will probably require sweeping or vacuuming at about that same rate!) During the rest of the year, the undercoat stays put, but the shepherd continuously sheds some outer guard hairs. The constant trail of dropped fur is so

German Shepherds come in a number of colors and combinations. The tan and black combination is the most common, while white shepherds are more rare. In the past, white shepherds were considered inferior, but today white is an acceptable color for a pet German Shepherd.

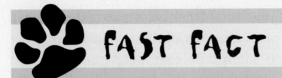

FAST FACT

When the German Shepherd breed was newer, all-white puppies were frequently born to dark-colored parents. Most German breeders and many American breeders killed the white pups at birth because they were considered defective and could not be registered or entered in shows.

characteristic of this breed that owners sometimes jokingly refer to their dogs as "German shedders."

German Shepherds come in a wide variety of solid colors and color combinations. Typical two-color dogs have a black saddle marking along their back and sides, with brown, cream, silver, tan, red, or sable on the rest of the body, the head, and the legs. German Shepherds of any color, including white, are welcome in Agility, Obedience, Rally, and other companion competition events. In the Conformation ring, however, dark, richly colored shepherds are generally preferred, and white dogs are disqualified. Any color German Shepherd will have the same loyal attitude, intelligent mind, easy trainability, and athletic body this breed is known for. So, unless you intend to exhibit in Conformation,

German Shepherd color is a matter of personal preference.

German Shepherds are so highly intelligent that they can figure out how to escape from almost any confinement if they really want to get out. They also have a well-developed sense of humor. Owners tell stories of jokes their German Shepherds have played on them and swear they've sometimes seen their dogs laughing at them. German Shepherds are observant, intuitive, and quite good at reading their owners' moods and responding to them appropriately.

The eyes of the German Shepherd are extremely expressive of the dog's moods. When he is happy, his eyes light up with joy. When he is sad, his dark eyes melt into pools of melancholy. When a shepherd is feeling

The owner of a German Shepherd can easily tell how her dog is feeling with a glance into the shepherd's expressive eyes.

playful, his eyes will beam with mischief and dog-laughter.

ROLES YOUR DOG MIGHT HAVE

German Shepherds make excellent pets and companion dogs for individuals or families because they enjoy being with their special person or people and naturally form bonds of deep loyalty. Beyond simple companionship, you and your German Shepherd might enjoy participating together in competition sports like Agility, Obedience, Rally, Tracking, Flyball, Freestyle, or Conformation.

If you do a good job teaching your German Shepherd what you want him to do, he will try his best to fulfill whatever role you ask of him. Shepherds excel as police and military service dogs, and they shine in civilian roles as well. German Shepherds, with their heritage as herders and guards, can quite easily fill the role of all-purpose farm or ranch dog, and some can even be trained to hunt.

Because of their physical stamina and natural intelligence, German Shepherds are often trained for police work.

German Shepherds serve admirably as guide dogs, hearing dogs, and assistance dogs for individuals with disabilities, as well as emotional-therapy dogs.

BEST ENVIRONMENT FOR THIS BREED

German Shepherds were originally bred to work all day, keeping large flocks of sheep safe from predators and moving them from pasture to pasture without letting any of the

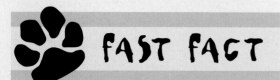

FAST FACT

The first American guide dog was a female German Shepherd named Buddy, who began guiding her blind master, Morris Frank of Nashville, Tennessee, during the late 1920s.

herd stray or dawdle. Today, German Shepherds retain that drive and strong sense of duty and responsibility. Shepherds love learning, thrive on being trained, and truly seem to enjoy performing the duties and tasks they've been taught to do.

German Shepherds need to interact closely with their human family or special person. In any type of home environment, good training will help the German Shepherd understand his owner's expectations and how to behave appropriately. No dog, not even the most brilliant shepherd, is born knowing all the rules.

Shepherds need to exercise and be active daily, with long walks on or off leash and vigorous free exercise like fetch games or swimming. After the need for exercise has been met, most German Shepherds are able to settle comfortably for relaxation time with the family.

The German Shepherd is a versatile dog, both in the type of work he can do and in the type of environment to which he can adapt. Many shepherds can live an equally content existence on a ranch or in an urban townhouse, as long as he has a useful job or task to do, a person to do it for, and proper exercise.

COSTS INVOLVED BEYOND THE PURCHASE PRICE

Regardless of whether you get your German Shepherd for free or pay a month's wages for him, that initial price is just the beginning of what your dog will cost. The price of maintaining a dog varies, depending on his age, how healthy he is, what food and services cost where you live, and what kind of lifestyle you choose for your shepherd. Here is a list of the basic yearly expenses necessary to maintain a German Shepherd. Keep in mind that as the cost of living changes, so does the cost of keeping a dog.

FOOD: $300 to $1,000. This depends on what type of food you choose to feed your dog. Foods with better-quality ingredients cost more to make, so they also usually cost more to buy, but better-quality foods are usually more nourishing, more palatable, easier to digest, and better for the dog's health and longevity.

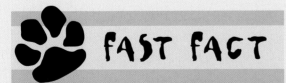

FAST FACT

German Shepherds are amazing escape artists. Shepherds have been known to figure their way out of a ten-foot (three-meter) high chain-link kennel with a securely fastened chain-link-panel top.

GETTING THE RIGHT STUFF

It is extremely easy to go overboard, spoiling your new German Shepherd with tons of toys and the nicest bed. However, shepherds have simple needs—something hard, yet soothing to the gums, to chew on, and a basic dog bed will suffice. (Although, if given the chance, he'll happily sleep on your bed!)

You will want to spend a bit more on his food and water bowls. Buy ceramic or metal bowls—plastic ones are cheaper, but bacteria can build up on plastic and this can lead to upset stomachs. Shepherds will also chew up plastic bowls, so you are better off investing in a good bowl right from the start.

When it comes to toys, make sure to buy toys that are durable. When looking for chew toys, check the package's chew meter. German Shepherds are strong chewers even as puppies, so pick toys with a high chew threshold. No toy is indestructible, so whenever you give your Shepherd a new toy, stay with him while he plays with it, especially if you suspect it may not last that long. If it comes apart, take the toy away so your Shepherd cannot ingest small, sharp pieces.

Don't give your shepherd toys he can easily chew apart, as these present a choking hazard.

VETERINARY CARE: $200 to $500. These costs reflect the price of well-dog care, including veterinary exams, immunizations, and protection from heartworm, fleas, ticks, and other parasites. Illnesses, accidents, or injuries will quickly multiply these amounts, often increasing them into the thousands of dollars.

TRAINING: $150 to $2,000. Training costs vary widely, depending on whether you sign up for private or group lessons and how much and what kind of training you decide to give your pet.

GROOMING: $50 to $800. This varies by whether you bathe and groom your shepherd yourself or hire a groomer to do it. The high-end of the price range is based on one professional grooming per month.

GENERAL EQUIPMENT: $100 to $600. This includes such everyday items as collars, leashes, food dishes, chew toys, beds, and bedding.

These basic costs add up to a minimum of $800 a year, but they could go much higher, depending on the cost of living in your area and

FAST FACT

An active 80-pound (36-kg) adult German Shepherd needs to eat approximately four cups (960 ml) of premium dry kibble food or two-and-a-half pounds (one kg) of fresh meat and bone each day.

where the shepherd fits into your family budget.

CHAPTER TWO

Breed History and Background

The German Shepherd originated in Germany during the late 1800s. The breeding stock that was used as the foundation for this strong, intelligent, and versatile breed came from working farm dogs whose ancestors, for centuries, had herded sheep and other livestock and kept them safe from predators and thieves.

Captain Max von Stephanitz, now known as the "father" of the German Shepherd, was the person primarily responsible for the formation and initial development of this breed. Von Stephanitz was a German cavalry officer with a passion for canine breeding and evolution. He was also a great admirer of the intelligence and ability of working sheepdogs. Von Stephanitz had a good eye for an attractive dog, but put the emphasis in his breeding program on qualities of intelligence and utility, rather than selecting dogs for their beauty.

The dog that began the German Shepherd breed and contributed strongly to the early gene pool was a working sheep dog named Horand v Grafeth. Von Stephanitz discovered this dog at a show and knew right away that here was the foundation dog for his new breed. Von Stephanitz wanted an easily trained dog with a strong work drive, one versatile enough to perform any kind of work he was taught to do. Horand v Grafeth seemed to embody all the qualities von Stephanitz sought in a dog.

In 1899 von Stephanitz, his friend Artur Meyer, and a small group of other interested men founded a national "parent club" for the German Shepherd, called Verein für Deutsche Schäferhunde ("Association for German Shepherds," abbreviated "SV"). Von Stephanitz was the first president of the SV and led the organization with a strong hand until 1935.

As the German Shepherd became known in the United States and other countries, the breed began to gain popularity. Breeders in each country formed their own national parent clubs and began holding exhibitions and competitions for the breed. In the United States, a parent club, the German Shepherd Dog Club of America (GSDCA), was founded in 1913.

During World War I (1914–1918), von Stephanitz saw his breed's versatility, strength, and courage tested under battle conditions. The dogs

German Shepherds were sometimes used as couriers during World War I. This dog is carrying a message from German soldiers stationed at an observation post.

shone in every job they were given. German Shepherds worked as sentry dogs, messenger dogs, guard dogs, and rescue dogs. Soldiers from the United States and the British Commonwealth recognized the German Shepherd's loyalty, bravery, intelligence, and versatility, and took some of the dogs home with them after the war.

THE SAD FATE OF GERMANY'S DOGS

With the onset of World War II, the world changed drastically for the German Shepherd. During the war, German Shepherds were used by both the Axis and the Allied forces, and earned great admiration for their wartime feats. This was the kind of dog many soldiers wanted for themselves when they returned to civilian life.

Meanwhile, many of Germany's dogs were injured or killed by bombings and gunfire, and hundreds more died at the hands of their owners. Wartime deprivation meant that there was barely enough food for humans to eat, so trying to keep a breeding kennel of large dogs well fed became an impossible task. Many German Shepherd breeders in Germany killed their own dogs to prevent the dogs from slowly starving to death.

By the time the war ended, very few good specimens of the breed were still alive in Germany. As a result, dogs from the United States and other countries were needed to rebuild the breed in its country of origin. But German Shepherds from countries outside Germany had begun developing notable differences in body and temperament from the German lines. The breed's recovery in Germany was a process of trying to regain its former qualities, and with such a small gene pool to work with, that recovery was more like a second founding of the breed.

FAST FACT

After World War I, when everything German was unpopular in the United Kingdom, the name of the German Shepherd was changed in Britain to the Alsatian Wolf Dog. In 1977, the name was changed back to German Shepherd.

SHEPHERDS GO HOLLYWOOD

Hollywood played a significant role in bringing the German Shepherd into the homes and hearts of America. In the days of silent films, two exceptionally handsome German Shepherds lit up the silver screen with their exciting and heroic adventures. First came Strongheart in

THE SAGA OF RIN TIN TIN

In 1918, during World War I, an American soldier named Corporal Lee Duncan found a five-day-old litter of pups and their mother hiding in the ruins of a bombed-out breeding kennel in Lorraine, France. He kept two of the pups, a male and a female, and other soldiers took the rest of them. Duncan named his puppies after a pair of tiny toy puppets that were popular good-luck charms in France at the time. He named the male pup Rin Tin Tin, and the female Nannette.

Duncan found out that the master who had been in charge of that breeding kennel, a German, had been taken prisoner by the Americans. Duncan got permission to visit the German in the American prison camp and he asked the man many questions about the German Shepherd breed and about the parents and ancestors of the pups he had rescued.

When Duncan returned home to Los Angeles after the war, he brought the two puppies with him. Sadly, only the male pup survived their 15-day ocean voyage to New York and then the long train trip across the United States to California.

After returning to civilian life, Duncan trained Rin Tin Tin and attended dog shows

The original Rin Tin Tin, Hollywood, 1925.

with him. The dog was brilliant, strong, agile, and handsome. Duncan decided to write a movie script for Rin Tin Tin and trained him for the role. Then he started making the rounds of Hollywood's film studios, trying to find a producer to make his movie.

Studio after studio turned down Duncan's script, but he refused to give up. Finally Duncan found a small studio, teetering on the brink of bankruptcy, which was willing to shoot and produce his script with Rin Tin Tin in the lead role.

The movie was a phenomenal hit with the public and Americans fell in love with Rin Tin Tin. The studio made over two dozen highly successful movies featuring Duncan's handsome and talented German Shepherd. During his film heyday, Rin Tin Tin received up to 10,000 fan letters a week and was considered one of the major stars in Hollywood. Rin Tin Tin passed away in 1932, at the age of 14.

Perhaps you're wondering about the name of the struggling film studio that daringly risked its dwindling resources to make a film written by an amateur screenwriter, starring a German Shepherd. That studio was Warner Bros. Pictures, and it staged a miraculous turnaround when it started making movies with the amazing Rin Tin Tin.

The Silent Call (1921), and then Rin Tin Tin in *The Man from Hell's River* (1922). Both of these dashing dogs starred in many silent films. When Hollywood finally began making "talkies"—movies with sound—Rin Tin Tin's bark was heard in numerous full-length features as well. The high-profile image of German Shepherds as hero dogs, cultivated by filmmakers, created a positive public feeling for the breed and sparked a desire among thousands of moviegoers to acquire handsome, heroic German Shepherds of their own.

From 1954 to 1959, *The Adventures of Rin Tin Tin* was a popular television show. By that time the original Rin Tin Tin was long gone, but several of his descendents carried on his wonder-dog role. Tuning in to the television adventures of Rin Tin Tin made Americans want to own German Shepherds, and the breed's popularity soared as a result.

The American Kennel Club, or AKC, registers more than 1 million purebred dogs each year.

BREED STANDARDS AND CONFORMATION

Each purebred dog breed registered by the American Kennel Club has a parent club, which is organized and led by experienced breeders and other fanciers of that breed. Each parent club develops a written description of the perfect dog of that breed, and this is the criterion by which dogs of that breed are judged in the show ring. This description is known as the Standard of Perfection, usually referred to simply as the "Standard." The Standard of Perfection always covers the proper appearance and gait, and many Standards also include a description of the ideal temperament of the

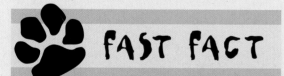

FAST FACT

In 1925, barely a dozen years after the breed was recognized in the United States, the German Shepherd leaped ahead of all other breeds to become number one in popularity.

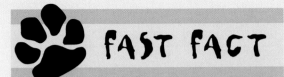

FAST FACT

White is not considered a permissible color for German Shepherds in the AKC Conformation ring, but white shepherds are allowed to compete in other events.

breed. Reputable breeders strive to produce dogs that conform to the Standard of Perfection as closely as possible.

While some Standards are brief and leave many details open to individual interpretation, the German Shepherd Standard describes the breed in great detail. But even the shepherd's finely detailed description leaves some room for interpretation. That's why shepherds from different breeding-kennel bloodlines often look strikingly different from one another. However, the German Shepherd should always be, as stated in the Standard, "a working animal with an incorruptible character combined with body and gait suitable for the arduous work that constitutes its primary purpose."

GENERAL APPEARANCE

German Shepherds tend to command public attention and admiration wherever they go. Large, muscular, and agile, the

German Shepherd has an alert carriage and an attentive expression. The appearance of this breed has long made it a popular artist's model for sculptures and paintings.

Male German Shepherds should stand between 24 and 26 inches (61 and 66 cm) tall at the highest point of the shoulders. Females are normally smaller than males, with their desired height range from 22 to 24 inches (56 to 61 cm).

A correctly built German Shepherd should be longer than tall, with the desired proportion of 10 inches (25.4 cm) in length for every eight-and-a-half inches (21.6 cm) in height. This proportion results not from having a long back but from the correct angulation and combined length of forequarters and hindquarters.

The German Shepherd has a noble appearance.

The German Shepherd's head has a strong and noble look. The male should look distinctly masculine, and the female distinctly feminine. The eyes are dark and almond-shaped and the ears are erect and moderately pointed. This gives the shepherd an alert, intelligent expression. The muzzle is long, strong, and wedge-shaped, the lips fit closely, and the nose is black. The jaws are strong and the teeth meet in a scissors bite, where the inner surface of the top incisor teeth is in contact with the outer surface of the lower incisors.

FAST FACT

Adult German Shepherds have 42 teeth—20 in the upper jaw and 22 in the lower jaw.

The German Shepherd's neck is muscular and without loose skin folds. The shoulders are strongly muscled and the withers (the highest point of the shoulders) should slope down to a strong, straight back. The croup (the area from the top point of the hip to the tail) is long and has a gradual slope.

The shepherd's tail is somewhat bushy but not fluffy, and should reach at least to the hock joints of the rear legs, though it is usually longer than that. The tail is normally held below the level of the back and carried in a slight saber curve. When excited, the shepherd may lift his tail above the level of his back, but it should never curl over the back.

The German Shepherd's chest is deep, so it has plenty of room for the heart and lungs to work well. The abdomen should be firm, not flabby or paunchy, and moderately tucked up in the loin area.

The German Shepherd's pointed ears and bright, expressive eyes are physical characteristics that help illustrate the breed's natural intelligence and alertness.

COAT AND COLOR

The proper German Shepherd coat is a medium-length double coat, with a dense layer of straight, coarse, outer guard hairs that lie close to the body. Under that is a layer of soft insulating undercoat fur. The undercoat should not be visible through the outer guard hairs. A straight outer coat is preferred, but a coat with a slight wave or a somewhat wiry texture is permissible.

The shepherd's neck fur is longer and thicker than the coat on the rest of the body. The hair on the head and face is short. The hair on the legs and paws is also short, except for the fur on the back of the thighs, which is longer and denser.

German Shepherds come in a fairly wide palette of colors, most of which are accepted by the Standard. Rich, dark colors are preferred, though, and pale or washed-out colors are considered serious faults.

GAIT

The German Shepherd is built to move effortlessly all day over any type of ground, covering a lot of territory with little effort, while herding or doing other work. The shepherd's strides are long, smooth, powerful, and rhythmic. This breed has a different style of trot than most other

The shepherd's coat has varying thickness depending on where it is on his body. Typically, the fur is thicker and fuller around his neck, while the fur on his paws and face is shorter.

dogs. At the fast extended trot there is a moment of suspension, where all four feet are off the ground at once and the dog almost seems to be floating in midair.

CHAPTER THREE

Responsible Pet Ownership

As the owner of a German Shepherd, you are morally responsible for his care and training. You are also legally responsible for any damage your dog might cause. Shepherds are among the breeds apt to be restricted by certain communities and by some homeowners' insurance companies. The German Shepherd is known as a guard and protector, and many people are fearful of large dogs. Shepherds that display bad manners or aggression are likely to be judged more harshly than smaller breeds. So shepherd owners must be exceptionally

You can easily look up your town's requirements for dog licenses online. Most towns, cities and municipalities have Web sites outlining licence procedures and requirements.

responsible: the public and the courts will hold them to a higher standard.

LICENSING REQUIREMENTS

Each state, county, and municipality has its own set of rules that dog owners living there must obey. One type of rule almost every urban and suburban community enforces is the licensing of dogs.

Licensing costs vary considerably, but almost all communities charge less—often significantly less—to license a spayed or neutered dog than an intact one. Unlicensed dogs, if picked up as strays, usually earn their owners a steep fine for failing to comply with licensing laws, plus the cost of buying a license. That means you'll need to abide by all licensing requirements in your area, and you should make sure to properly identify your dog in case he gets lost or stolen.

IDENTIFICATION

Proper identification on your dog is important for his own safety and your peace of mind. If your German Shepherd were ever lost or stolen, good ID could be the key to getting him back. The three main types of ID are collar tags, tattoos,

FAST FACT

Pet theft is a real issue. The National Dog Registry estimates that in the United States, about one in five dogs will become lost or stolen at some point.

and microchip implants. A DNA profile is another type of ID that is increasingly used with show and breeding dogs, but has not yet reached the pet-dog sector. There are pluses and minuses to each of these identification methods, so having more than one type of ID for your dog is a good idea.

COLLAR TAGS

A plastic or metal ID tag fastened to your shepherd's collar, with your contact information engraved on it, is a good first line of defense.

It's a good idea to get a collar with sturdy fasteners to ensure that it doesn't fall off your dog.

Make sure your German Shepherd has a tag with the proper contact info while vacationing. Should your dog get lost, whoever finds him will be able to reach you during the trip.

Anyone finding your dog can easily read the tag and contact you directly. For security reasons you may choose not to list your name, your dog's name, or your home address on the tag, but it should include at least your home and cell phone numbers and perhaps your email address. It's wise to list your city and state of res-

idence on the tag as well, so the finder can figure out how far from home your dog is.

When vacationing with your dog, have a tag made that includes the phone number where you are staying and the number of a contact person your dog's finder could reach in your absence. If there's no time to get a separate tag engraved with your vacation contact numbers, write them in waterproof pen on a piece of cloth adhesive tape, and stick it on top of his regular tag.

The drawback of tags is that they can be lost or purposely removed, leaving no ID on your dog at all.

TATTOOS

This means of identification usually consists of a string of numbers and/or letters applied in permanent ink on the dog's inner thigh. The procedure takes only a few minutes and the sensation ranges from tickly to slightly painful, depending on the dog's sensitivity and the skill of the tattoo artist. The plus side of tattoo identification is its permanence; you can use it to prove that the "found" dog is yours. The downside is that the ink may fade over time, and the characters may stretch as a dog grows, making the tattoo difficult to read.

There are tattoo registries that, for a fee, will keep a record of your dog's tattoo number and your contact

Having your shepherd tattooed is another identification option. The green ink on this pup's right ear shows that he was recently tattooed.

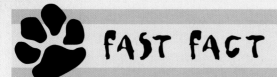

FAST FACT

If you want a permanent, fail-proof identification method for your dog, consider having a profile made of his DNA. The American Kennel Club has a DNA profiling program that enables your dog to be identified by his genes.

information. Many people finding a dog would not know to look for a tattoo, however, and even if they did find it, they couldn't contact you directly to reunite you with your dog.

MICROCHIPS

This form of identification is a small computer chip the size of a grain of wild rice. The chip is implanted under the skin between the dog's shoulder blades, through a special large-bore needle. Each microchip is coded with a unique number, which is registered to the dog's owner through one of several microchip registries. If someone finds your lost German Shepherd, the staff at nearly any veterinary clinic or shelter in North America should be able to scan the dog's back with a special microchip reader. Your contact information will come up, and you will be contacted and reunited with your shepherd.

SPAYING AND NEUTERING

Should you neuter your shepherd? For several decades, neutering pets by removing their reproductive organs has been the politically correct thing to do. According to the Humane Society of the United States, every year more than 3 million unwanted dogs are euthanized in animal shelters. The practice of spaying females or neutering males is intended to reduce this problem by preventing the birth of unwanted pups.

There are other good reasons to consider spaying or neutering your pet. Removing your shepherd's reproductive organs will eliminate some undesirable sexually driven behaviors. Intact male dogs are more likely to roam away from your property, especially if there is an intact female in the neighborhood. They also have a stronger tendency than their neutered counterparts to mark their territory with urine, or to develop aggressive behaviors such as "humping" the legs of visitors. Spaying a female shepherd eliminates her estrous cycle (commonly known as being "in heat"). Intact females typically experience a messy discharge of blood during their heat cycle. Spaying before the first heat cycle also eliminates the risk of ovarian or uterine cancer, infections of the uterus, and other diseases associ-

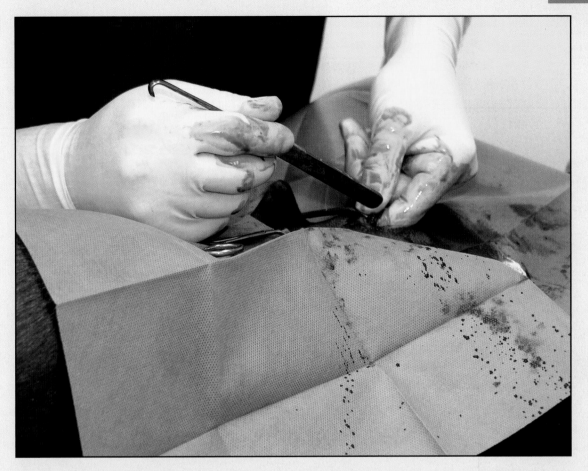

Choosing whether or not to spay or neuter your dog is an important decision. While there are some health benefits, if you have a purebred German Shepherd you won't be able to compete in Conformation events if he has been neutered.

ated with the female's reproductive organs. Spaying also reduces the risk of mammary tumors.

However, in recent years counter-arguments have surfaced against neutering pets. Those who oppose spaying or neutering dogs point out that responsible owners can fairly easily confine their dogs to prevent unwanted litters. They also note that although some puppies are put to sleep, most dogs euthanized at shelters are adolescents or adults relinquished by their owners, not baby pups that couldn't find a home. In addition, in recent years some of the supposed health benefits of neutering have been called into question or proven to be false. For example, it was once believed that neutering would protect male dogs against prostate cancer. However, recent

LEGAL ISSUES

Owning a large, powerful, protective dog like a German Shepherd means you may face legal issues that owners of smaller breeds never encounter. Some towns and cities have laws restricting certain dog breeds, and the German Shepherd is sometimes among them. Your shepherd may have to be muzzled in public, or he may have to have a particular leash length. Special fees or licenses may be required as well.

General nuisance laws in your community may or may not have a provision addressing dog ownership in particular, but dogs that bark incessantly, whether indoors or out, are considered a nuisance. Don't leave your dog unattended outside to bark and disturb your neighbors. If your dog is an inveterate barker, you should

Depending on where you live, your shepherd may be required to wear a muzzle when out in public.

find ways to train him to eliminate this behavior.

Know the laws and regulations in your area and the places you might travel with your dog, so you and your shepherd stay legal and free.

studies have indicated that castrated males may actually have a higher risk for prostate cancer than intact males do. Nonetheless, neutered male dogs are much less likely to develop other common prostate problems as they age.

There are pros and cons to neutering, and dog owners need to educate themselves about both sides of this issue to make the best choice for their own shepherd. But in light of recent studies on the effects of neutering, and with more studies in progress, neutering can no longer be considered the only responsible option for canine population control.

PET INSURANCE

You can decide to purchase pet insurance, which will cover the bills if anything serious happens to your German Shepherd, such as an accident or a serious health condition like cancer. Pet insurance means that you don't have to make the difficult decision between treating your dog and putting him down because the treatment is too expensive. Several brands of pet health insurance are available, and the right coverage could save you thousands of dollars in veterinary bills.

Health insurance for your German Shepherd can be a huge financial help if he encounters serious medical problems, but there are numerous exclusions—procedures and tests the typical policy won't cover—so buyer beware. For the most part, annual vet visits, vaccinations, and elective procedures such as teeth cleaning or spaying/neuter-

FAST FACT

A dog's owner can be held legally responsible for property damage done by the dog.

ing are not covered by insurance policies. Preexisting medical conditions, and diseases common to the German Shepherd breed like dysplasia, are often excluded from these policies. Before purchasing a policy, read it carefully so you understand exactly what it covers.

CHAPTER FOUR

The Best Possible Beginning

While all German Shepherds share certain traits—or they wouldn't be German Shepherds—no two individual shepherds are exactly alike. Some of them will be the kind of dog you're looking for, while others will have traits that don't appeal to you. Here are some tips to help you find a German Shepherd that will be a good match for you.

FACTORS TO CONSIDER

Male or female? Some people believe that male shepherds are more affectionate or make better guards than

When choosing a shepherd, consider your family, lifestyle, and the size of your home. Doing research and making an informed choice will be best for everyone.

females, but these traits are not linked to gender. Both male and female shepherds can be equally affectionate and equally serious in their approach to their designated duties.

Male Shepherds are typically taller, more muscular, and stronger than females, and the male head is usually larger and broader. Some people are attracted to that larger size and the stronger, more masculine appearance, so they choose a male. Other people prefer the slightly smaller size and feminine look of the female shepherd.

Most adult German Shepherds make friends more easily and get along better with dogs of the opposite sex than with dogs of the same gender. This is especially true for intact (not spayed or neutered) shepherds. If you already have a shepherd and are getting ready to add another, consider the way your current dog behaves around other dogs of the same sex. If he or she doesn't get along well with same-gender dogs, save yourself a load of frustration and perhaps prevent some dogfights by opting for a second dog of the opposite sex.

If you want your German Shepherd to serve a special purpose, such as search and rescue or police service, it may be in your best interest to find a breeder whose shepherds' bloodlines have a history of service.

When you are considering acquiring a German Shepherd, choosing one will be easier if you have some idea about what you'd like your dog to accomplish. Are you interested in participating in competitive sports, like Obedience, Agility, Tracking, or Herding? Would you like to exhibit your dog in Conformation shows? Would you like to get involved in pet-assisted therapy by bringing your German Shepherd to hospitals and nursing homes? Are you looking for a dog to help out around your farm and keep predators away from your livestock? To find a good candidate, seek out breeders whose dogs have proven their potential in the sports or activities that interest you most.

Structure, temperament, and talent can all be inherited, passed down from parent to pup. Good training

FAST FACT

If you have an obviously purebred German Shepherd without registration papers, and would like to compete in Agility, Obedience, or other AKC events, you can do that. Apply for an Indefinite Listing Privilege (ILP) and AKC will issue your dog a number that will allow you to enter him in these competitions. The ILP willl not qualify your shepherd for Conformation shows, however.

and the right kind of stimulation can strengthen and enhance a dog's inherited potential, but to excel in a particular activity, the potential must be present from the beginning. You will be more likely to find that potential in a pup whose parents and other relatives demonstrate that ability already. If you have a specific sport or activity in mind for a German Shepherd you are considering, but are fairly new to that activity yourself, have someone with experience evaluate the pup or dog before you make the final decision.

HOW TO FIND A RESPONSIBLE BREEDER

The German Shepherd Dog Club of America (GSDCA) has a Breeder's Code, which is a voluntary code of ethics and excellence in breeding practices. The Breeder's Code serves as a guideline for the breeding and sale of German Shepherds. Members of GSDCA who sign on to the code promise to maintain the highest possible standards of health, cleanliness, and care of their German Shepherds. This includes physical care, such as proper diet, exercise, and veterinary treatment, as well as psychological care, such as training and proper socialization.

The Breeder's Code requires all dogs considered for breeding to first be x-rayed for hip and elbow abnor-malities. Breeders provide their puppy buyers with complete health records for their pup, a four-generation pedi-gree, and the proper paperwork to register the dog. A puppy or dog from a breeder who adheres to the GSDCA Breeder's Code should be clean, healthy, and confident. You'll have a better chance of finding a responsible and reputable German Shepherd breeder if you choose from among those who are members in good standing of GSDCA and have signed on to the Breeder's Code.

ADOPTING FROM A SHELTER OR RESCUE ORGANIZATION

Another option is adopting a dog from a shelter or a rescue organiza-tion. Many lovely German Shepherds, through no fault of their own, are relinquished to shelters and rescue organizations. Dogs are given up for adoption for many reasons, most commonly because of changes in the owner's situation. A parent gets a job in a new town and the fam-ily cannot take the dog with them. A child in the family develops an allergy to the dog. The owner dies and no one in the family wants his dog. Some dogs end up in shelters or res-cue organizations because the previ-ous owner couldn't work with their behavior or temperament, but most

of them are there not as rejects but as victims of circumstance. You can find wonderful German Shepherds in shelters and rescue organizations, and one of them might be the perfect companion for you.

When you adopt a dog from a shelter or rescue organization, there may not be much information avail-able about his past. Ask the person handling the adoption to tell you as much as possible about the dog's behavior while he was in their care.

If you are considering getting a German Shepherd, a good option may be to adopt one from a local shelter or rescue organization. Hundreds of perfectly wonderful dogs are sur-rendered to shelters each day. Your local shelter or rescue organization may just be holding your new best friend.

If you are not very experienced with shepherds, when you go to meet the dog you are thinking of adopting, take someone with you who has experience with this breed. If you don't have an experienced friend, consider hiring a dog trainer to evaluate the potential adoptee. Make sure the trainer understands the qualities that are important to you, so she helps in picking the right dog.

But even after gathering all the information you can about the dog and heeding the most expert advice, you can still get some surprises after you've had your new dog for a few

BREED RESCUE ORGANIZATIONS

Breeders and others who love German Shepherds volunteer their time, talents, and resources to help homeless shepherds through nonprofit rescue organizations. Some canine rescue organizations are small, independent, local groups, while others are larger and better organized, with national and regional associations closely connected through a network of volunteers. There is a strong rescue network for German Shepherds.

Rescuing German Shepherds can be expensive when you consider the high cost of veterinary care, food, transportation, equipment, phone, mailing, and hundreds of other miscellaneous needs. Funds raised to help offset these costs are used up quickly, and more money is always needed.

The American German Shepherd Rescue Association (AGSRA) is a fundraising and educational organization that offers grants to groups that rescue German Shepherds from abuse, neglect, homelessness, and cruelty. Animal-loving philanthropists will sometimes donate a large sum to a rescue organization. Most of the money for operating rescue groups is raised by the volunteers themselves through bake sales, garage sales, auctions, dog-walkathons, and whatever other fundraisers they can think of to bring in needed donations.

Rescue groups are always looking for more volunteers, and there are jobs for anyone willing to help. Rescue organizations need volunteers to foster adoptable dogs, groom and exercise dogs, organize fund-raisers, do home checks of prospective adopters and make follow-up visits after adoptions, help with paperwork and office chores, or even make a couple dozen cupcakes for a bake sale. Any assistance you can give to your local or regional rescue group is appreciated, and everything you do helps homeless German Shepherds.

months. Newly adopted dogs are often on their best behavior for about three months after the adoption. By that time the dog will have settled in and gotten confident in his new home, and may start relaxing and behaving differently. Sometimes those "new" behaviors are really old habits that got the dog into trouble with his previous owner.

Puppies are sometimes found in shelters or rescue organizations, but most of the dogs found in these places are adolescents and adults. When you adopt a dog that is past puppy-hood, he may already be housetrained and know some obedience cues and other good skills. These are some of the benefits of

FAST FACT

The best way to keep your dog from exhibiting unwanted old habits is to enroll him in a training class and help him establish good habits for his new life with you.

adopting adolescents or adults. But if you're totally set on adopting a German Shepherd puppy, you may have to wait a while to get one from a shelter or rescue organization. Buying a pup from a breeder, on the other hand, may entail a shorter wait.

WHAT TO LOOK FOR IN A PUPPY AND ITS PARENTS

When you go to look at puppies, have in mind the temperament and personality you'd like your dog to have. It's easy to be instantly captivated by every pup—they're all so cute. But not every pup will be right for you, so don't fall for the first pair of sweet brown eyes that gaze into yours with a look of love. Handle and observe the pups for a while and then decide if one of them is destined to be yours.

By seven weeks old, a pup's natural personality and attitudes are fairly easy to recognize if you know what to look for. You can learn a lot

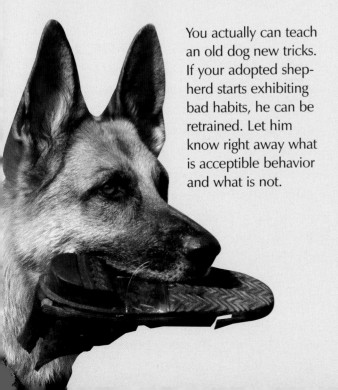

You actually can teach an old dog new tricks. If your adopted shepherd starts exhibiting bad habits, he can be retrained. Let him know right away what is acceptible behavior and what is not.

their actions. This shows you how each pup approaches unfamiliar situations.

Observing pups at play can give you a pretty good idea of how curious and how bold they are, and where they stand on the "social pushiness" scale. As they mature, pups tend to keep the same personality and temperament, so imagine a grown dog exhibiting those traits and that will help you decide which pup would best fit your needs.

If the parents of the pups or any adult relatives are available, take a look at them, too. Puppies grow up resembling their relatives, so characteristics of physique and temperament that you see in the adults, you may also see in your pup when he matures. If you plan to enter your shepherd in competition events, seek out a litter with parents that are accomplished in the events that interest you. Dogs with talent and drive are likely to produce offspring with the same qualities.

Performance dogs for Agility, Obedience, Conformation, and other competitive sports tend to do best if they are curious, bold, and

Think about what type of personality you'd like your dog to have. Do you want a high-energy, aggressive dog, or would you prefer a shepherd with a more mellow or quiet personality? Watch the litter of puppies and see how they interact, then play with them individually to find the right dog for you.

about puppies by watching how they play with each other. See how they interact with their littermates and note which pups tend to be bossy and which get bossed around. Place a large object, like an open cardboard box, in their play area. Some pups may explore it, some may ignore it, some may run and hide, and some may wait and watch what the other pups do and then mimic very persistent. Not everyone wants or needs a dog like that. People who want dogs mainly as companions usually prefer less intense dogs than people who train them for competition in performance events.

CHOOSING A VETERINARIAN

Next to you, the veterinarian is your dog's most important ally in maintaining good health over his lifetime. If you don't already have a veterinarian for your pup, you need to find one and schedule a wellness exam. Don't wait until your dog really needs a veterinarian; instead, arrange for him to meet the veterinarian during a period of normal health. German Shepherds are often wary of strangers, so meeting the veterinarian under pleasant conditions will help your shepherd accept being handled by the doctor during future visits.

To find a good veterinarian for your German Shepherd, start by asking your dog-owning friends and acquaintances, especially those with large dogs, which veterinarians they use. If several friends like the same veterinarian, that's a good sign.

Another sign to look for is the one on the veterinarian's reception counter that says "AAHA." That stands for American Animal Hospital Association, an educational organiza-

tion that helps those in veterinary practices to uphold the highest standards of animal care and accredits those clinics that meet them.

Time is usually of the essence when a dog gets sick or injured, and if the veterinary clinic is far away, the trip to the clinic can use up precious time better spent with the doctor. So if you have a choice between a veterinarian who is within a fifteen-minute drive and one who is an hour

When choosing a vet, look for the AAHA logo (above). Veterinarians who are members of the AAHA are held to a higher standard than those who aren't members.

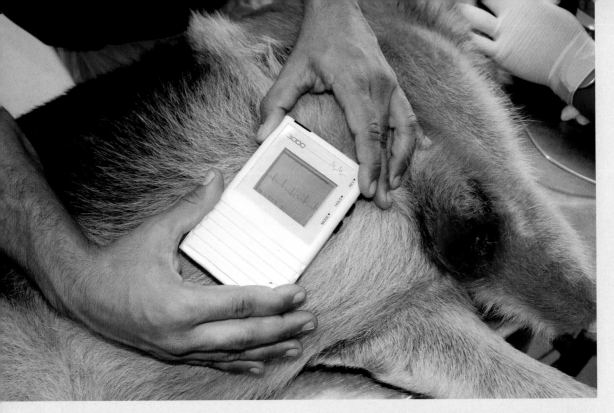

Depending on your veterinarian's hours, you may need to find a clinic where you can take your German Shepherd in case of an emergency. Here, a vet monitors a shepherd's heart before surgery at an emergency clinic.

away—all else being equal—it makes more sense to opt for the closer one.

Take into consideration whether your veterinary clinic is open twenty-four hours a day. If not, you'll need to make arrangements in case a medical emergency occurs during off hours. Find out what your veterinarian's policies are for handling off-hour emergencies. Some rural veterinarians will rush from home at any hour and open the clinic for a patient with a true emergency, but that kind of service is rare and vanishing fast.

In some places, local veterinarians form an alliance to handle off-hours emergencies, each taking a turn on call overnight and on weekends and holidays. Many urban and suburban areas have emergency veterinary clinics that stay open 24/7, or clinics that only open during off hours.

Once you have lined up one or more veterinarians who sound good, plan a visit to the animal hospital for an interview and a hospital tour. Make an appointment for this and pay for the vet's time. Veterinarians are usually very busy, and any time they spend answering your questions is time they would otherwise spend with animal patients.

CHAPTER FIVE

Caring for Your Shepherd Puppy (Birth to Six Months)

Before your new puppy comes home, you'll need to get your home and family ready for the new arrival. Establish the rules for the pup before you bring him home, and make sure all household members, including children, understand the rules and the reasons behind them. People often follow rules better if

they help come up with them, so ask family members for ideas and suggestions for parameters for the pup.

Puppies explore their surroundings by playing with and chewing whatever draws their attention. Their avid curiosity can be destructive or even dangerous, however, if your home has not been puppy-proofed.

German Shepherd puppies love to chew things and will make quite a mess unless you prepare your home properly.

A pup's angle on the world is different from yours; he views everything from closer to the floor. To put yourself in his paws, get down to puppy-eye level and take a look around. Anything that sticks out or hangs down will immediately attract a pup's attention, which means he'll probably chew on it. Remove those things or block your pup's access to them. Don't just make it challenging for him to reach dangling objects—shepherds enjoy meeting challenges. Make it impossible.

PAPERS THE BREEDER WILL PROVIDE

When you buy a purebred German Shepherd that can be registered, the breeder should give you all the paperwork necessary for registration when she sends the dog home with you. If you don't get all the paperwork when you pick up your shepherd pup, it may be more difficult to get it later.

Here's the paperwork the breeder should give you when you get your puppy:

- The application form she got when she registered the litter, so you can register your pup individually.

- A four-generation pedigree

- The dog's vaccination and health records, including microchip and/or tattoo identification numbers, if applicable.

If the dog is an adult, the breeder should sign his registration over to you as his new owner.

WHAT TO EXPECT THE FIRST FEW MONTHS WITH YOUR PUP

On the first night home with a new pup, neither your family nor the puppy will likely get much sleep. The puppy is used to sleeping with his littermates, so the first night without them he may whine or howl a sad lament.

To ease that loneliness, let him sleep in a crate or a pen in your bedroom. The pup will

Your pup may be sad and lonely the first night you bring him home. Let him sleep near you so that he doesn't feel completely alone. In time, he will adjust.

take comfort from being able to see, hear, and smell you and won't feel so lonely in the unfamiliar surroundings. If you received a piece of clothing or small blanket from the breeder when you picked up your pup, put it in the crate with him. The scent of his mother and littermates will give him additional comfort. If you wrap a warm water bottle in a towel, your puppy may snuggle with it the way he did with his littermates. It also helps to play soft background music when you put the pup to bed. The music will soothe him so he'll be able to fall sleep—eventually.

PUPPY HEALTH

Hopefully, your puppy will be healthy when you get him, because once he enters your care, it will be up to you to keep him that way. Keeping a dog healthy takes work, but it's easier and less costly than treating a serious disease or injury. Make sure your pup gets what he needs for good health, including clean water, nourishing food, daily

When you take your German Shepherd to the vet, be sure to remember his health records so the veterinarian has a clear understanding of your dog's medical history.

exercise, timely immunizations, and regular veterinary exams.

Although some veterinary clinics do accept walk-in clients, most will require an appointment to see the doctor. When you get to the veterinary clinic, leave your dog in the car, if possible, while you check in at the front desk. There will be paperwork to fill out for the new patient's file, and that will be easier without an excited or worried pup on your hands.

Bring along the health records the breeder gave you as well as any medical information you have on your puppy's parents. The doctor will be asking questions regarding your pup's medical history, and that information may be important.

When you check in, ask if the vet's appointments are running on schedule. Sometimes your veterinarian may get tied up with an emergency, so caring for that animal becomes the top priority. That emergency case will take time that wasn't scheduled and the day's appointments may start running late.

If you arrive early or find that an unscheduled emergency is causing a delay of more than fifteen minutes, keep your dog outside. He will probably stay calmer and be more comfortable if you sit in the car with him or take him for a walk instead of the two of you hanging around the wait-

ing room. Be back in the clinic at least five minutes before your pup's turn with the veterinarian. Any time you leave the waiting area, tell the staff where you'll be, in case the doctor is ready sooner than expected.

WHAT TO EXPECT AT A VETERINARY EXAM

When the veterinarian examines your pup, she will run her hands all over him. She will palpate his abdomen, checking for hernias, muscle tone, and any lumps or irregularities. She will feel his legs, hips, and elbows, and check for signs of dysplasia (a hereditary malfor-

A good veterinarian will give your pup a thorough examination. If she finds anything that concerns her, she may recommend further testing.

mation of the hip socket and/or the top of the thigh bone; see pp. 75–76), tenderness, or stiffness. She will check the pup's skin for lumps, bumps, flea dirt, or anything else that doesn't belong there. She will listen to his heart for murmurs and check the sound of his lungs. She will examine his ears and eyes and check his hearing and vision. She will look in his mouth and throat, and examine his teeth.

While the veterinarian examines your pup's body, she will also observe his personality and degree of socialization. If she thinks your pup needs more socialization or practice with body handling, she may suggest ways to do that or refer you to a trainer or behavior specialist who can teach you what to do and help you do it.

If your puppy has not been wormed or if he shows any signs of parasites, such as frequent unformed feces or a habit of rubbing his butt on the floor, take a fresh fecal sample to the veterinarian so it can be checked under the microscope. Only a small amount of feces is needed for that; a sample the size of a thimble is plenty.

VACCINATIONS

Recent scientific studies have radically changed the thinking about

VACCINATION SCHEDULE FOR PUPPIES

The following vaccination schedule is recommended by the American Animal Hospital Association:

Vaccine	Age of Puppy
Distemper	8 weeks and 12 weeks
Parvovirus	8 weeks, 12 weeks, 16 weeks
Parainfluenza	8 weeks, 12 weeks
Coronavirus	8 weeks, 12 weeks
Canine adenovirus-2	8 weeks, 12 weeks
Leptospirosis	8 weeks, 12 weeks
Bordetella*	12 weeks
Lyme disease*	12 weeks, 16 weeks
Rabies +	16 weeks

* Optional vaccines, depending on location and risk.   + Required by law.

Source: American Animal Hospital Association

Newborn puppies don't open their eyes until they are about 10 to 14 days old. During this crucial time, the mother dog provides protection, warmth and nourishment by feeding them breastmilk. Eventually, they can start to be weaned off breastmilk, and puppy food can be introduced into their diet.

canine immunizations. Veterinarians used to recommend immunizing all dogs once a year against every disease for which a vaccination existed. That protocol is being overhauled as this book goes to press, as major veterinary schools are calling for a new policy of fewer vaccinations, less frequent boosters, and tailoring an immunization protocol to the individual needs of each animal.

At this point, some veterinarians are still following the old vaccination protocol, while others have switched over to the new one. The best approach for a dog owner is to keep up with the news in this area. Until a consensus is reached on the best vaccination protocol, follow the guidance of the veterinarian who knows your dog best.

PUPPY NUTRITION

A German Shepherd puppy needs a balanced diet of easily digestible foods, rich in high-quality proteins and fats, and containing all the vitamins and minerals needed to nourish his rapidly growing body. The mama dog's milk meets all these requirements in the pup's first few weeks.

As each pup is born, the dam (mother dog) first washes and stimulates him by licking him off, then she guides the pup to a teat and he starts nursing. The mother's early milk contains colostrum, which transfers to the puppies the mother's immunity to diseases for which she has been vaccinated. This maternal immunity lasts until the pups are between two and four months old, protecting the litter from dangerous viruses until they are old enough to receive vaccinations themselves.

The dam nurses her puppies until their baby teeth have grown in, and many mama dogs continue nursing for several weeks after that, even though those needle-sharp teeth hurt her teats when the pups nurse. When the pups get to be five or six weeks of age, their dam will have trouble keeping up with their appetites and the breeder will need to start weaning them onto soft solid foods, like baby cereal or ground meat thinned to a gruel with water.

When puppies first start lapping up this food, they usually end up wearing as much of it as they swallow. Over the next few weeks, the dam's milk supply dwindles and she nurses less often. Soon the pups will be fully weaned onto solids.

In their natural state, dogs eat mainly meat and bones, though they can digest other foods as well. A rapidly growing German Shepherd puppy needs plenty of protein and fat for healthy growth and energy. Your pup can get the nutrients he needs either from a premium commercial dry food or from a diet of fresh meats, bones, and organs. Another alternative is frozen dog foods, which are convenient for dog owners who don't have the time or inclination to make balanced, home-prepared meals

for their dogs. Frozen blends of fresh ground foods, formulated to supply most or all of the nutritional components a healthy dog needs, are sold at many pet food stores.

There is no one "best" diet for puppies or dogs. People have strong preferences when it comes to dog food, but dogs can do well on a number of different diets. Between you and your veterinarian, you should determine the diet that your dog thrives on, and that's what you should feed him.

FEEDING SCHEDULE

Puppies need a lot of nutrients to keep up with their rapid growth

Many pre-packaged dry foods have been scientifically formulated to provide your growing puppy with all the important nutrients he needs. By doing a little research, you can decide which brand or kind of food will be best for your dog.

spurts. That, plus all the energy pups expend playing and exploring, makes it crucial for puppies to refuel frequently. Feed your pup at about the same times each day, spaced apart fairly evenly. The younger your pup, the more times a day he will need to eat. Be sure to pick up his bowl when your dog is done eating. This will establish the feeding regimen and keep his diet on track.

From weaning to about ten weeks of age, your puppy needs at least four meals a day. From ten weeks to about four months, the pup will need to eat three times a day, plus maybe a light snack at bedtime. From four or five months through one year of age, your pup will need two meals a day, and that same routine can continue through the rest of the dog's life.

Though most adult dogs can stay healthy eating only one daily meal, most are more comfortable being fed twice a day. Dividing your dog's daily ration into two smaller meals will help keep him from feeling overly hungry as mealtime approaches. Also, two smaller meals mean there is less in the dog's stomach at any one time. This is a sensible way to feed a German Shepherd, as it helps reduce the chance for bloat, a painful and potentially dangerous disorder fairly common in this breed (see page 76–79).

COGNITIVE DEVELOPMENT AND SOCIALIZATION

As the days and weeks go by, your shepherd pup's brain will be growing and maturing, just as his body is. Your pup will begin to understand how his world works and how to make it work better. He'll have a longer attention span, he'll figure things out more quickly, and he'll be able to learn more new skills and do more with what he knows.

Socialization is one of the most important things you should do to prepare your shepherd pup for adulthood. The more people, animals, and new situations a pup encounters by the time he reaches maturity, the more confident, savvy, and accepting he'll be as an adult. Be careful, however, that the number of people and things you introduce to him doesn't overwhelm your pup. Figure out how much he can handle, and avoid push-

FAST FACT

Behavior acquired early in life is quite durable. Teach your shepherd puppy polite manners, and he'll grow into a well-behaved adult.

ing him past that point. Socialization training helps the pup discover that the world is a friendly place and that the people, animals, and situations he will encounter are interesting but harmless. Overwhelming him with too much at once may backfire badly and create fear, instead of dispelling it.

Introduce your puppy to between three and five new, friendly people a week. The people should represent as many varieties of human beings as possible. Let your pup meet tall, short, old, and young people. Introduce him to men with facial hair; women with big hats; kids on skates, scooters, and boards; runners and hikers; bicyclists and motorcyclists; folks of all sizes, shapes, and colors. Make sure the people he meets are friendly and gentle, and don't let them do anything to frighten him.

If you want your shepherd to be protective of your family and property, it's just as important to socialize him to lots of friendly strangers. He'll learn that when you want him to be friends with someone, you'll purposely introduce him. He'll view those people as friends because you're there telling him they are and making sure they stay friendly. When he matures he will recognize the difference between people you tell him are friends and people who sneak and trespass and behave very differ-

Socializing your puppy will help him learn how to behave appropriately in many different scenarios.

ently than "friends" do. Socializing your shepherd will make him a better, more discerning and intelligent protector than if he distrusts all people outside the family.

Socialization includes introducing your pup to friendly dogs, cats and other pets, and large animals like horses, cows, and llamas. For the animal socialization, choose carefully, because if an animal you deem

Introduce your pup to people and animals in and around your home.

When it comes to animals other than dogs, it's often safest to let the pup see, hear, and smell them but avoid physical contact, particularly if the animals are not yours and you don't know if they'll be gentle with pups. Go near enough to them for your pup to satisfy his curiosity but far enough away so everyone stays safe.

Some people avoid taking their pups out to socialize and meet the world until they have all their shots. Unfortunately, by that time the main window of opportunity for socializing a pup has usually passed, and the pup has developed an ingrained fear of the unfamiliar. To socialize a puppy that's been isolated most of his first six months is a longer and more complicated process.

GROOMING

German Shepherds shed huge quantities of fur during their twice-yearly coat changes, each of which generally last a month or more. To keep your shepherd looking tidy, and to reduce the amount of loose fur clinging to your clothing, carpets, and furniture, you'll need to brush your shepherd every day while he's shedding, and twice a week year round.

Your puppy's coat is soft and wooly compared to the coat he'll have as an adult. His adult coat will

"friendly" intimidates or hurts the pup, he may lose faith in your ability to distinguish safe from unsafe.

A Puppy Kindergarten class is a great place for your shepherd pup to meet and play with other dogs his age. You and the class instructor will both be there to make sure the puppies have fun and no pups bully others. Playtime and lesson time alternate in a good Puppy Kindergarten class, so your pup will learn to listen to you, even if several of his puppy pals are nearby.

Your puppy's crate will serve as his home inside your home. Make sure it is large enough for him to easily stand up, turn around, and stretch out.

keep him warm and dry in nasty weather, but his puppy coat won't. Until your shepherd's soft puppy fur is replaced with the weather-resistant double coat of an adult, you'll need to protect him from wet, chilly weather with a sweater and dry his head, coat, and feet thoroughly if he goes out in the rain.

DENTAL CARE

Clean teeth and healthy gums are important to your German Shepherd's overall health. When a dog's teeth become caked with hardened plaque and the gums become infected, bad breath is the least of the concerns. Food residue that remains on teeth after eating promotes the growth of bacteria and the formation of plaque, which will make the dog's breath smell unpleasant and irritate his gums. Irritations can lead to infections, and bacteria from those infections can find their way into the bloodstream and travel to the heart. If that bacteria in the bloodstream infects

Keep your shepherd's teeth and gums healthy by brushing them regularly. This will keep your dog happy and healthy, and may reduce "dog breath."

the dog's heart valves, serious illness or death may result.

Some dogs can keep their teeth fairly clean by chewing on bones or chew toys, but often that's not clean enough for optimal dental health. Brushing your German Shepherd's teeth daily can help prevent plaque buildup, so that would be a good habit to get into. Once plaque has hardened, you may not be able to remove it by brushing. When this happens, the dog should have his teeth cleaned by the veterinarian.

Many dogs need professional teeth cleaning annually, and some need cleaning twice a year. Keep an eye on your dog's mouth. If you see a hard whitish, brownish, or yellowish buildup on your dog's teeth at the gum line, schedule a professional cleaning.

BATHING

Dogs do not perspire through their skin the way humans do, which is why dogs don't develop a sweaty odor after exercise and why they don't need to bathe as frequently as we do. The natural oils in a German Shepherd's coat do give the coat a slight odor that intensifies with time, heat, and moisture. Those oils also pick up and hold dirt and grime from the environment, which can lend a sticky feel to the coat and add to doggie odor. Thorough brushing of your shepherd's coat, several times a week, will keep him looking and smelling acceptable, but no matter

how often you brush him, he'll eventually need a soap-and-water bath.

Though some old-timers insist that dogs should not be bathed more than once or twice a year, more frequent bathing is not harmful. In fact, baths keep your dog's skin and coat clean, and that's good for him. It will make him feel better to be clean, and a pleasant-smelling dog with a clean, shiny coat is more likely to attract positive attention

Bathing your German Shepherd at home can be a big undertaking. If you aren't sure you can handle the job, there are many dog grooming companies that offer bathing and grooming services at a reasonable cost. Some even have mobile units that will come to your home, saving you the trouble of transporting your dog to the facility.

and affection from people. These are good things.

Many dogs dislike baths, but your dog doesn't have to look at it that way. You can make bathing less distasteful—and even pleasant—for your dog, if you go about it the right way. Here are some tips to help you accomplish that.

Prepare the tub by placing a nonskid rubber mat on the bottom, so your dog will have good traction and not hurt himself by slipping and sliding.

Keep the drain open and don't fill the tub. Dogs usually prefer this to standing in slippery, soapy water.

Take a couple dozen small yummy treats into the bathing area with you, and dole them out to your shepherd every few minutes during the bath.

Wet down your dog's coat with wrist-temperature water (cooler than people usually like for bathing), using the shower wand or a plastic pitcher.

Put about a quarter-cup (60 ml) of shampoo in a gallon (4 liter) jug and fill the jug with lukewarm water. Use this diluted shampoo as the soap for your shepherd; diluted shampoo will be much easier to work into his fur than full-strength shampoo. Also, you will use less shampoo this way and it will take less time and water to rinse it out of the coat.

Apply the shampoo and lather it through the coat, starting at the neck and working toward the tail. Keep your dog's head and face dry until the end of the bath, and any time water is splashed on his face, quickly wipe it off with a dry towel. Once the dog's head gets wet, he will want to shake it off, and waiting until the end to wash his head and face will keep you drier during the bathing process.

Rinse your dog, starting with the head and working back toward his tail. Rinse him until the water running down the drain is clear and has no more bubbles. Then rinse him one more time. If you leave any shampoo in the coat, it will attract dirt and become sticky and stinky, and your dog will need another bath much sooner than he would otherwise.

Dry your shepherd as thoroughly as possible with towels, then finish the job with a blow dryer set on low or cool. If you don't use a hair dryer, it will take hours for your shepherd to dry all the way to his skin. In warm weather this is not generally a problem, but if you let him go outside in cool weather before his undercoat is completely dry, he can get a bad chill.

NAIL CARE
Your shepherd's nails need to be trimmed regularly or they will grow

excessively long and sharp. Not only can long toenails deliver a nasty scratch, but they can start growing in a curve that will tend to get snagged on things and be torn off. This is very painful for the dog, so avoid that possibility by making it a habit to trim your dog's nails frequently.

Nail trimming should optimally be done every week, but a trim every two weeks can still keep a shepherd's nails in good shape. If you let it go longer than that, though, the blood vessels and nerves in the living tissue (called the "quick") inside the nail will grow out too close to the end of the nail. This will make it difficult to trim your dog's nails without nicking the quick and causing the dog pain.

You can trim your dog's nails with special scissors or clippers made for pet nails. If you don't feel confident

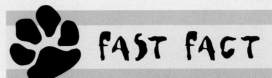

FAST FACT

It may be a good idea to keep a few treats on hand when trimming your shepherd's nails. Many dogs dislike having their feet handled, especially by someone holding a clipping device. Speak calmly, and reward your dog with praise or a treat when he lets you clip him. By showing your dog there is no reason to get upset, he will learn in time that nail clipping is nothing to fear.

using tools with blades on your dog's nails, you could file them down by hand instead with a convex file for dogs' nails. If that's too slow for you, try shortening your shepherd's nails with an electric rotary tool, similar to those used in nail salons.

To trim the nails, support the dog's paw and steady the toe you're working on. Trim off just the tip of the nail. Don't cut too much off, or you'll hurt the dog. If you cut too deep, you'll nick the blood vessels that feed the nail, causing bleeding and pain. Commercial blood coagulant powders are available at pet-supply

With practice, you'll learn how to keep your shepherd's nails trimmed to the right length.

CANINE FIRST AID

When a dog joins your family, it's important to have canine first aid supplies on hand. Your canine first aid kit should contain the following items:

- gauze pads
- antibiotic ointment
- hydrogen peroxide
- petroleum jelly
- eye wash
- ear wash
- medications
- bismuth tablets
- sterile stretch gauze
- bandage scissors
- splints

- a blanket
- tweezers
- tensor bandage
- rectal thermometer
- paperwork, including the dog's health record
- medications
- local and national poison control numbers
- phone numbers for your regular veterinary clinic and the emergency clinic.

stores. These powders will quickly stop a nail from bleeding when it's cut too short. Buy some and keep it on hand, just in case.

Show grooming for a German Shepherd is really no different from ordinary day-to-day grooming. Some breeds take all day to get ready for the ring, but a bath, a thorough brushing, and a quick nail trim are all a German Shepherd needs.

TRAINING

All dogs need to learn the manners required for living with humans.

Teaching clean elimination habits is one of the first training challenges you'll face with your pup, but you can make housetraining easier by establishing a consistent routine. Put your pup on a regular eating schedule and he will have more predictable elimination times. Give him frequent opportunities to use the designated potty area, and that will help prevent messy accidents in the house.

Teach your shepherd a cue word or phrase for elimination. Pick something you won't be embarrassed to say when out in public. Popular

Housetraining a shepherd puppy isn't easy. It will take patience, practice, and time. Remember, your shepherd doesn't know it's not okay to eliminate indoors, so he may not understand why he's being put outside so often. He must be taught that elimination must only be done outside. Eventually, your shepherd will catch on.

cues are "Go potty," "Do business," or "Hurry up." Say the cue when your pup is in the area you want him to use. Wait patiently until he goes, then quietly and calmly praise him.

When your pup has potty accidents—and all pups do—don't scold or punish him. Scolding can make your pup avoid you when he has to eliminate, but he needs your help to get outside.

If you see your pup start to eliminate indoors, call his name, clap your hands, or say something to get his attention. Then tell him, "Outside! Potty outside!" and quickly escort him to the approved area. At the potty place, calmly encourage him to eliminate, and then praise him when he does.

If you don't catch your pup in time and you discover a potty accident after the fact, get a paper towel and take the pup back to the accident spot. Don't scold or shame him, just calmly blot up the pee or pick up the poop in

THE POTTY BELL

One common cause of housetraining accidents is a pup's inability to let his people know when he needs to go outside. You can resolve this issue easily by teaching your pup to ring a bell when he needs to go outside to eliminate.

Hang a bell on a cord and tie it around the handle of the door closest to your pup's outdoor potty area. You won't have to teach your pup to ring it; just ring it yourself before opening the door each time you take him out to eliminate.

Your pup will soon make the connection between the bell ringing and the door opening, and will wonder if the bell causes the door to open. Within about a week after you start ringing the bell, he will give it a try himself. When he does, praise him and open the door for him. Once he realizes that he can "make" you do that by ringing the bell, he'll use it whenever he needs to go out.

the paper towel, then gently escort your pup to the elimination area. Smear the pee or drop the poop there, then step back and calmly praise your pup, "Good potty outside," as you would if he had gone there to begin with. Your puppy will learn that there's a "good place" to do potty business, and with your help and patience he will learn to use that area.

ESTABLISHING HOUSEHOLD RULES

The best time to establish household rules is when you first get your pup. Don't allow your puppy to do things you wouldn't find acceptable in an adult shepherd. If you start with one set of rules now, and then try to change them when your pup gets older, that will confuse him. It's harder to change an ingrained habit than to establish a good one, so think about how you'll want your

FAST FACT

If you catch your pup in the process of eliminating in an improper place, do not punish him. Just interrupt him and escort him to the right place.

Set the ground rules early, be consistent, and don't be afraid to be firm with your dog. If you don't want your adult shepherd sitting on the furniture, never let him sit there as a puppy. The key is to teach him good habits while he's young.

German Shepherd to behave as an adult, and help him learn those behaviors while he's young and impressionable.

FAST FACT

Children follow rules for their shepherd pup better when they're allowed to help devise those rules. Include your children in the rule-making process about what the pup is allowed to do and how the pup should be treated.

If, for example, you allow your pup to sit on furniture, he'll want to lounge there as an adult. If you're sure that will be okay with you, go ahead and invite him onto the couch. But if you don't want an adult shepherd on your sofa or bed, set that rule while your pup is young and stick to it.

Consistency is one of the hallmarks of good training technique. Make sure you give your shepherd pup consistent guidelines to follow, and enforce the rules you set up fairly.

CHAPTER SIX

Things to Know As Your Shepherd Grows

From six months to two years of age a German Shepherd develops from an awkward, long-legged, adolescent into a graceful, well-proportioned adult. During this period, the dog's bone growth slows and then stops, and the bones finish hardening.

HEALTH ISSUES

Every breed has some health conditions that occur more frequently than average among other dogs. Some of these conditions are hereditary, while others are just related to the breed's size or shape. Here are

As your shepherd grows, you will begin to see his personality develop and mature.

some conditions that tend to affect dogs in this age group.

PANOSTEITIS: Panosteitis, or "wandering lameness" is found mainly in large and giant-breed dogs under two years old. A growth condition of the leg bones that can cause lameness, it will often move from one leg to another, then suddenly disappear, and then days or weeks later return just as suddenly. Most dogs with panosteitis make a full recovery with or without treatment.

EXOCRINE PANCREATIC INSUFFICIENCY: Another problem that affects German Shepherds is exocrine pancreatic insufficiency (EPI), a genetic condition that causes a gradual deterioration of the part of the pancreas involved in protein digestion. Your dog may have this condition, which first appears in puppyhood, if he steadily loses weight and muscle, even though he has a voracious appetite and eats large quantities of food. (For more information, see page 80.)

EPI is hereditary and there is no cure for it, but in most cases it can be managed by giving the dog powdered pancreatic enzymes at mealtime. The enzyme supplement aids digestion, so the dog regains the lost weight and his elimination returns to normal.

PARASITES: Dogs should be checked for internal parasites at least once a year. If that hasn't been done since your dog was tiny, you should take in a fecal sample and have the veterinarian check for worms again. Young pups, elderly dogs, and unhealthy dogs all tend to build up large populations of various worms in the digestive tract. Worms seldom bother healthy, strong adults, but your shepherd should be checked and given deworming medicine, if needed.

External parasites like fleas prefer dining on weakened individuals, but they wouldn't turn down a blood meal from almost any warm-blooded creature. If you see evidence of fleas on your shepherd—frequent scratching, chewing on the rump at the base of his tail, or dark red or blackish "dirt" in that same area—give your pet a flea bath as soon as possible. Most flea collars aren't very useful on large dogs, but several brands of the liquid

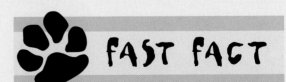

FAST FACT

If you see dark red or blackish "dirt" on the skin of your dog's rump, it may be flea feces. To find out, drop a few grains of it into a tablespoon of water. If the water turns red, that's your shepherd's blood in the flea poop.

anti-flea treatments that are applied to the back of the dog's neck or withers are good on dogs of any size. Veterinarians generally stock and dispense the various brands of these flea treatments, and several of these products are also available, without prescription, from dog supply stores and catalogs.

HEARTWORM: Heartworm is a serious health problem for dogs in most areas of the United States, but it's worst in moist, warm climates with large populations of mosquitoes. As its name suggests, heartworm is a worm that lives in the heart.

Mosquitoes carry heartworm. When a dog is infected with heartworm, a microscopic immature stage of the heartworms (called microfilaria) circulates through the dog's bloodstream. If a mosquito bites the infected dog, along with its blood meal it draws in some microfilaria as well. If that mosquito bites another dog, some microfilaria will be injected into that new victim, where they will continue their life cycle and in about three months migrate into the heart itself and develop into adult worms. Within six to eight months, these adults are beginning to reproduce, adding more heartworms to the dog's growing load.

Each adult worm can reach a length of 12 inches (30.5 cm) or more. If a tangle of these worms clogs a dog's heart, it cannot pump efficiently, so the dog becomes weak and sick. A heavy load of heartworms, left untreated, will lead to the dog's death.

Administering prescription medications that kill the microfilaria before they develop into adult heartworms can prevent heartworm infection. The preventive must be used just before mosquitoes appear in spring until they go dormant for winter. In some parts of the country, mosquitoes stay active year round, so dogs must remain on preventive heartworm medication all year long. Your veterinarian can advise you on the best preventive regimen for your area.

Before your shepherd is given a heartworm preventive, he must be tested to make sure he is not already infected. It can be fatal to administer preventive heartworm medication to a dog with adult heartworms. A

FAST FACT

Dogs should be checked for internal parasites at least once a year. Take a small fecal sample to your veterinarian and have it examined for microscopic worm eggs.

THE DANGER OF HEARTWORMS

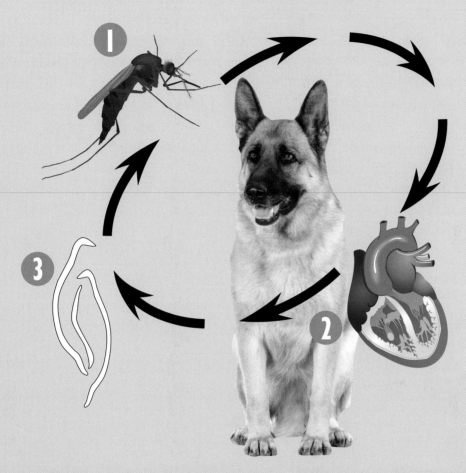

Heartworms are a concern for all dog owners. The graphic above illustrates the cycle of heartworm development. When a mosquito (1) bites a dog, it can inject microfilaria into the dog's bloodstream. The microfilaria travel through the bloodstream to the heart (2), where they grow into heartworms (3) and multiply, clogging the dog's heart. If left untreated, heartworms can kill.

different regimen is needed to clear up a heartworm infection.

VACCINATIONS

If you followed your veterinarian's protocol during your pup's first six months, your shepherd should be finished with vaccinations for the year. Many veterinarians suggest yearly boosters for all vaccinations, though studies currently in progress show that yearly boosters may be unnecessary, and they can be hard on some dogs' immune systems. The advice you follow about vaccination schedules should come from a veterinarian you trust.

NUTRITION

Your shepherd is heading into adulthood at this stage. By one year of age he has reached his adult height, but he is still building muscle mass, so he still needs nutrition for a growing dog. His food should be rich in highly digestible forms of protein and fat, as well as vitamins and minerals, for muscle-tissue growth, overall health, and high energy.

Pick a high-quality food that is made for large-breed dogs. Cheaper foods contain too much fat or vegetable protein, and this can lead to rapid growth. Another problem with feeding your shepherd food that has lower-quality ingredients is that vitamin and mineral deficiencies can cause skeletal complications, such as hip or elbow dysplasia.

Your dog's stomach is now large enough for him to be fed all the nutrition he needs in two meals a day. If he likes a bedtime biscuit, he can certainly have that, too. As long

VACCINATION SCHEDULE (6 MONTHS–ADULT)

The following vaccination schedule is recommended by the American Animal Hospital Association:

Vaccine	Age for Boosters
Distemper	1 year, then every 3 years
Parvovirus	1 year, then every 3 years
Parainfluenza	1 year, then every 3 years
Coronavirus	1 year, then every 3 years
Canine adenovirus-2	1 year, then every 3 years
Leptospirosis	1 year, then every 3 years
Bordetella *	1 year, then as needed
Lyme disease *	1 year, then prior to tick season
Rabies +	1 year, then every 3 years

* Optional vaccines, depending on location and risk.
+ Required by law. Some states still require annual boosters.

Source: American Animal Hospital Association

as he's eating the right food, not overindulging on treats, and getting plenty of exercise, you won't have to worry about him getting too fat.

SOCIALIZATION

Socialization should not end when a pup is no longer little and cute. For best results, socialization

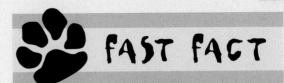

FAST FACT

A galloping German Shepherd can easily run a mile in three minutes. Don't turn your shepherd loose to run unless you're sure he'll come to you the instant you call.

should continue throughout his life. If you just adopted a shepherd in this age group that has not been well socialized, you can still do it, but socialization gets more complicated with age. An adolescent or young adult shepherd that hasn't met many people in his life will probably be somewhat shy, and shepherds tend to hide that "weak" emotion behind a show of dramatic, aggressive, loud barking. A shepherd not used to other dogs will put on the same kind of front. Unfortunately, all the adrenaline the dog works up doing that fierce show of aggression might make him decide to actually bite the one he is barking at so relentlessly.

A fearful fuzzy puppy that barks and growls to seem brave may look cute when he acts like that. But that same behavior in a 60-pound or 70-

At close to one year old, your shepherd is well on his way to adulthood. Choose a food especially made for large-breed dogs. If you're unsure what to get, ask your veterinarian.

The importance of socializing your German Shepherd doesn't decrease just because the dog no longer looks like a puppy. In fact, this period from adolesence into true adulthood is a critical time in shaping your pup's personality. The only way to avoid an out-of-control adult dog is to continue to reinforce principles taught in his earliest stages.

pound (27-kg or 32-kg) young adult is very scary—it's not cute at all, and most folks won't volunteer to help you convince your aggressive "Po-leece Dog" that strangers are friendly, nice people. If you need help working with a dog like this, you'll probably need to hire a professional trainer who understands that this type of aggressive display is fueled by fear. And you need to realize that just because he's afraid doesn't mean he won't bite. In fact, aggression prompted by fear often leads to bites.

So if your shepherd got a good start on socializing when he was younger, keep it up. Don't let him lose that good foundation you—or a previous owner—worked so hard to build.

PROPER EXERCISE

By six months your German Shepherd is more than half his adult size and will have the energy of two adults. At this stage he needs vigorous exercise every day. Not just a walk around the block on a leash at your pace, but running free, at his own speed, somewhere with room for him to stretch his legs and gallop.

Make sure that wherever you let your shepherd run for exercise is far away from traffic and other hazards.

German Shepherds need lots of exercise. If you don't have an extremely large backyard in which your dog can run, look into finding out if your community has a dog park. It's important, however, that you train your shepherd to respond immediately to your commands before you take him to an area where he'll be off the leash.

Galloping shepherds travel from here to there very fast. Don't turn your pup loose if he doesn't reliably come when you call, even when faced with alluring distractions like deer or ATVs. If he's a free spirit that doesn't respond to your call, he'll have to content himself with exercising in fenced areas.

TOO THIN OR TOO FAT?

German Shepherds under two years old naturally tend to be on the thin side. This sometimes worries owners, but it's normal for the breed. Many shepherds don't fill out until around three years of age. So if your young adult shepherd is healthy and energetic but leaner than you'd like, he probably just hasn't reached maturity yet.

If your young adult shepherd is thin enough to worry you, have your veterinarian examine him. If his lean body is normal for his age and development, your veterinarian will tell you so. If she thinks your shepherd needs to gain weight, she will suggest healthy ways to help him put on some pounds.

BASIC OBEDIENCE TRAINING

Start teaching your puppy good manners and obedience the day you bring him home, and continue this training for life. Dogs learn the rules of life by paying attention to what works and what doesn't. You are training your dog every time you interact with him, whether or not you're thinking about training.

If you have not yet taken your shepherd to obedience school, don't wait any longer to enroll in a class. By this stage in your dog's life he already thinks he knows how life works. Get him into training soon

German Shepherds are intelligent dogs and enjoy learning. While training your shepherd, keep him on a leash until you're sure he will return when you call him.

and teach him that wonderful things come to good shepherds that do as they're told.

To find trainers, ask for recommendations from your veterinarian and your friends who have trained their dogs. Training classes can be a lot of fun if you like the instructor and her methods. When you get some leads on trainers near you, call them and make arrangements to observe one of their classes without your dog, so you'll see how they relate to both two-legged and four-legged students.

TRAVELING WITH YOUR DOG

German Shepherds quickly become seasoned travelers, even at a young age. Most shepherds enjoy car rides so much that if you leave your car door open in the driveway, you may find your dog snoozing on the back seat, waiting for his personal driver to arrive.

Traveling with your German Shepherd can be a lot of fun, as long as you take precautions to keep him safe and comfortable.

Shepherds that are used to short car rides don't seem to mind longer trips at all. On a long road trip, most German Shepherds enjoy the changing scenery and sleeping in a new place each night. Shepherds are adventurous dogs, and any adventure is fun for them. They can even handle weeklong car trips, as long as they get a chance to hop

BOARDING KENNELS, PET SITTERS, AND DOGGIE DAY CARE

When you must travel and leave your shepherd behind, there are several care alternatives to choose from. If you have friends or relatives who are willing to take good care of your dog, you might be able to leave him with them or have them come stay at your home. That would be a great solution.

However, many people don't have friends or relatives able or willing to take on that responsibility. In that case, there are pet sitters for hire who will visit your dog two or more times a day, feeding, exercising, grooming, and even medicating the dog, if necessary. Some pet sitters will stay overnight at your home and care for your pets almost the way you would. They charge more for that kind of service, but for some dog owners—especially those with multiple pets—whatever the overnight sitter charges is worth the cost.

If you're away for long days all week and don't have much time or energy to exercise your dog when you get home, consider doggie day care. At day-care facilities, dogs are dropped off in the morning and picked up later the same day. Some day-care centers have vans to pick up the dogs and take them home, saving the owners that trouble.

Keep in mind that dogs with aggressive attitudes toward either people or other dogs are not good candidates for doggie day care. It will be stressful for them to be around non-family humans and dogs all day, and they will escalate the stress level of everyone else, both human and canine. Dogs that get along well with others can have a lot of fun at day care, however. Dogs that like people but not other dogs may enjoy being walked, petted, and played with by the staff.

Boarding kennels are mainly for overnight stays, though many offer doggie day care as well. Most boarding kennels keep the dogs in runs or cages most of the time, walking them on leash for a bit of exercise or turning them out into a fenced area to walk around and sniff on their own. A dog that dislikes other dogs may not do well at a kennel, unless his run is blocked visually from a view of other dogs. A dog that isn't good with people may fare better at some kennels, but it depends on how skilled the staff is in dealing with that type of dog.

The Web site of the National Association of Professional Pet Sitters, www.petsitters.org, can be used to help you find the right person to watch your pet while you're away.

out at rest stops to stretch and sniff around.

Travel in a car is usually more to a dog's liking than being crated in the cargo hold of a jet, but shepherds that have flown a few times settle into their flight crates calmly. If you plan to fly with your dog, check around with different airlines. At least one major airline has an extra-safe program for flying live animals, and its baggage handlers are specially trained for that. Airlines will not fly dogs when they consider the weather too hot or cold, because the animals might not withstand the flight in the hold without temperature control. Flights that both depart and arrive at night or early morning are the best flights for animals in warmer weather because those are the coolest times.

FAST FACT

Dogs should never be left alone in a vehicle, especially in the summer. The car's temperature can quickly rise, causing your shepherd to have a heatstroke. If he is not given immediate medical attention, death is likely.

CHAPTER SEVEN

Caring for Your Adult Dog

Your mature German Shepherd should see his veterinarian at least once a year for a well-dog examination. The veterinarian will take your dog's temperature and listen to his heart and lungs. She will look into your dog's eyes and ears, examine his mouth, teeth, and gums, and feel his body all over for lumps, swellings, or anything else that might indicate an injury or health concern.

In between these yearly examinations, if you notice anything that makes you suspect that your German Shepherd isn't completely healthy, you should consult with your veterinarian immediately. An alert dog owner can help the veterinarian keep

Your shepherd's general appearance will tell you a lot about how he's feeling.

a dog healthy by picking up early signs of illness and seeking medical help before the problem worsens. Some early signs of illness include:

- changes in energy or activity level

- changes in elimination habits or appetite and amount of water consumed

- uncharacteristic moodiness, grumpiness, or sensitivity to touch or sound.

These kinds of changes don't necessarily mean your dog is sick, but they might, especially if you observe several suspicious signs within the same week.

Many illnesses are preventable with healthy feeding, proper exercise, and good general care. There are some health issues, however, that a dog can be born with or might be genetically predisposed to develop. Responsible dog breeders have all their animals tested for any genetic abnormalities before breeding. The following sections discuss some disorders and diseases that often appear in German Shepherds.

HIP AND ELBOW DYSPLASIA

These structural abnormalities of the hip and elbow are found in many large breeds, including the German Shepherd. Hip dysplasia is a malformation of the hip socket and/or the top of the femur (thigh bone). Elbow dysplasia results when a small bone in the elbow fails to fuse properly during puppy-hood. Both abnormalities can be crippling and painful or just uncomfortable, depending on how much the bone is deformed and if bone rubs against bone whenever the dog moves.

Dysplasia is hereditary, but can be made worse or better, depending on the care given to the growing pup. Overfeeding and excessive exercise can both worsen these conditions, so it is best to keep pups on the lean side and be sensible about exercise.

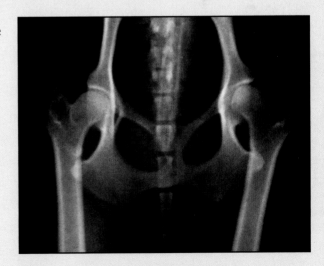

An x-ray of a canine pelvis. Hip dysplasia is hereditary, so if you intend to breed your dog, he must be genetically screened for the disorder.

Responsible breeders always x-ray their dogs' hips and elbows before they make the decision to breed them. The x-rays are sent to the Orthopedic Foundation for Animals for evaluation, and the dog's owner can use the results to determine whether his dog is sound enough to breed. As the practice of x-raying dogs for dysplasia before breeding them has grown more common, the incidence of these disorders has begun to go down. However, because of the complex genetic blueprint for dysplasia, it is unlikely that x-ray evaluation of breeding stock will ever completely eradicate these disorders.

BLOAT AND TORSION

The technical name for bloat with torsion is Gastric-Dilatation Volvulus (GDV). This condition occurs most frequently in deep-chested dogs over 40 pounds (18 kg). The German Shepherd is one breed that runs a higher-than-average risk for bloat and torsion.

Bloat involves the rapid formation and buildup of large quantities of gas and foamy mucus in the stomach. Bloat has a sudden and unpredictable onset and progresses rapidly. The pressure of the gas causes the stomach to expand inside the abdominal cavity and press against the heart, lungs, and abdominal blood vessels. The bloated stomach impinging on internal organs restricts their function and creates a painful and terrifying situation for the dog. Bloat can quickly become a life-threatening emergency, particularly if it's accompanied by torsion.

Torsion is a rotation of the stomach that pinches off its entrance from the esophagus and its exit through the duodenum. This traps water, food, gas, and foam, causing the stomach to swell even more. The blood builds up carbon dioxide because the inner abdominal pressure prevents the heart and lungs from doing their jobs of cleansing and oxygenating the blood. The dog's blood pressure drops, his body becomes toxic, and the stomach continues to become painfully distended.

The effects of bloat and torsion can kill a dog in under an hour. Bloat is an emergency that requires immediate veterinary intervention, especially if it seems to be progressing into torsion, a common occurrence. If you think your dog is having an episode of bloat, head for the veterinary hospital right away.

Call before leaving home and let the veterinarian know that you are on your way with a dog suffering from bloat. Then load your dog in the car and drive! Don't dawdle; the

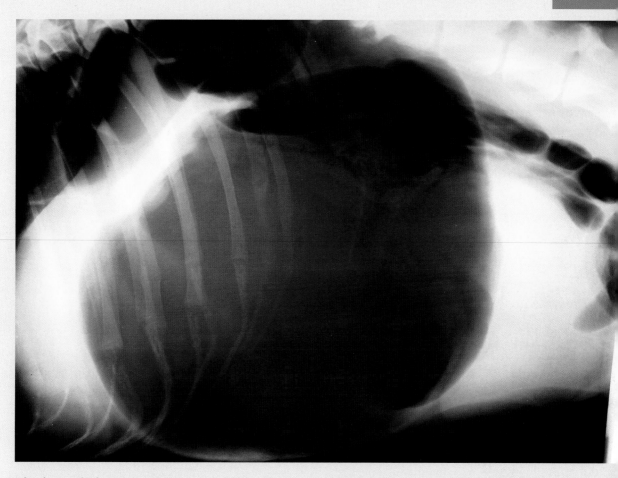

The large dark area in the center of this x-ray is gas trapped in a German Shepherd's stomach. Bloat is a very serious affliction; if you notice your dog exhibiting symptoms of the disorder, get him to a veterinarian immediately.

veterinarian may need those precious minutes to perform emergency surgery to save your dog's life.

When a dog comes in with bloat, the veterinarian will attempt to relieve the pressure by passing a large tube into the stomach by way of the mouth. If there is torsion, the tube will not get past that blockage and the only way to save the dog is to make an incision through the abdomen and into the stomach, so the gas can escape.

Once the pressure is relieved, the veterinarian can reposition the stomach. Dogs that bloat once will usually bloat again. To prevent torsion, the veterinarian will "tack" the stomach to the muscles around the ribs, using surgical sutures, so the stomach cannot twist out of position if the dog bloats again.

The causes of bloat are not yet known for certain, though there seems to be a hereditary predisposition for it in certain dogs, and a number of possible environmental and situational triggers.

Gulping air while eating may be one cause, so slowing down a fast eater can help. So can feeding him two smaller meals a day instead of one big meal. Stress may be a contributing factor, so keeping your shepherd calm and content may help prevent this condition.

For several decades it was widely believed that elevating food and water bowls to the dog's chest height would help prevent bloat. However, a study by veterinarians at Purdue University showed that elevating the

Keeping your shepherd's bowl on the floor can help reduce the likelihood of bloat.

WARNING SIGNS OF BLOAT

Your dog may try to vomit repeatedly; bloat is a possibility if nothing comes up, or if just blood and mucus are produced.

The dog will suddenly start to appear uncomfortable, whining, pacing, sitting up, or getting back down in an effort to eliminate the discomfort. The dog may not be able to rise, or may refuse to lie down.

Obvious abdominal pain and/or distention of the dog's stomach. The abdomen may feel tight, like the skin of a drum.

Heavy salivating or drooling.

The dog may start to go into shock. Symptoms of this include pale gums, an elevated heartbeat, and irregular, shallow breathing.

food bowl nearly doubles the likelihood for bloat.

Several antacid remedies made for human use contain an ingredient called simethicone, which can help slow or reduce the gas building up in a dog's stomach during a bloat episode. Always keep one of those products in your dog's first aid kit, so it's accessible immediately if your dog starts to bloat. It can be given to a large dog in the same dosage as recommended for people. If you can slow down the expansion of gas in your dog's stomach, it may mean less pain for your dog and it will slow

somewhat the dangerous progression of bloat into torsion.

DEGENERATIVE MYELOPATHY (DM)

This progressive neurological disease affects the spinal cord, causing a gradual loss of mobility. The symptoms begin in the hindquarters and progress from there. DM appears with relative frequency only in German Shepherds. It usually starts in dogs over seven years old, so the affected dog may have produced offspring before diagnosis of this often-hereditary disorder. For that matter,

Shepherds with Degenerative Myelopathy (DM) may require special care, but that doesn't mean they are any less fun!

the offspring and the offspring's off-spring may also have produced pups by that time, so the genes are already in the pool. There is no cure for DM, but there are supportive treatments—involving exercise, vita-min supplements, and medication with aminocaproic acid—to make the dog more comfortable.

EXOCRINE PANCREATIC INSUFFICIENCY (EPI)

This treatable but incurable disorder of the gastrointestinal tract might only occur in German Shepherds, and generally appears first in puppy-hood. The most common symptom is severe weight loss. A dog with EPI may pass large amounts of soft, unformed feces and many tend to eat their own feces as well as other non-food items. Not all dogs with EPI exhibit these signs, but may instead have bouts of intermittent vomiting and watery diarrhea.

In this disorder the pancreas does not produce the digestive enzymes needed to absorb nutrition from food. A strictly controlled special diet and supplemental digestive enzymes must be maintained for the dog's entire life or he will start losing weight rapidly. The special diet and enzymes are fairly expensive, but they're necessary to keep the dog from wasting away. This disorder may also cut years off the normal life expectancy of the dog.

PANNUS

This is an inflammation of the corneas in both eyes, which can sometimes lead to blindness. Pannus appears mainly in German Shepherds and shepherd mixes over two years old. Treatments for pannus are steroids and/or surgery.

VON WILLEBRAND'S DISEASE

This hereditary bleeding disorder is caused by a deficiency of a plasma protein necessary for proper clotting of the blood. It occurs in many breeds, including the German Shepherd. The condition is diagnosable with a blood test. It cannot be cured, but your veterinarian can treat excessive bleeding with special hormones or blood-clotting medicines. Dogs of any breed affected by Von Willebrand's disease should be tested for this disorder before being bred.

CANCER

There are many types of cancer—a disease that occurs when cells multi-ply uncontrollably, destroying healthy tissue—and some are more deadly than others. Cancer seems to strike almost randomly, in that it is difficult to predict and its causes are not always well understood. Certain can-after other treatments. When some types of cancers are detected early, the dog has a good prognosis for successful treatment and recovery.

The best way to detect cancer early is to be alert to any changes in your dog's body or health that might indicate that something is awry. As you pet your shepherd, let your fingers wander over his body. Lumps, bumps, and slow-to-heal sores sometimes signal cancer. If you feel something unusual, take a closer look and keep an eye on that spot for a week. If you notice any sores, clean and care for them. If they don't heal within a week, or if any lumps don't go away in that time, consult your veterinarian.

Bad breath can originate from dirty teeth, but it may also be a sign of a serious health concern, including cancer. Sudden onset of foul breath usually indicates indigestion. But if your shepherd's breath always smells bad, have the veterinarian examine him. If the doctor suspects anything beyond indigestion, she may suggest blood and/or urine tests to rule out more serious health problems, including cancer.

If your dog has a sore that he just won't leave alone, call your veterinarian. Sores that do not heal may be a sign of a more serious condition.

cers tend to run in families, but variables such as diet and stress may affect an individual's risk.

Different cancers are treated with different types of medical intervention. Treatment may include the surgical removal of tumors, radiation, and chemotherapy. Dietary supplements may be prescribed to strengthen general health both during and

EXERCISE

An adult German Shepherd needs daily exercise to stay healthy and maintain a positive mood. Lack of

It's important for your shepherd to get plenty of exercise in order for him to stay fit and healthy.

workout and uses all his muscles. Regular daily exercise builds stamina and muscle condition without over-taxing the dog's current strength or endurance. Sitting idle all week and then exercising to exhaustion on the weekend is as unhealthy for your dog as it is for you. That all-or-nothing weekend-athlete approach to exercise can cause strains, sprains, and other injuries that may be slow to heal.

To stay fit and prevent the onset of flab, your German Shepherd needs a daily minimum of two brisk, one-mile (1.6-km) walks plus at least a half-hour of vigorous off-leash exer-cise like swimming, fetching, or run-ning with dog pals. For continuing good health, your dog needs at least this much daily exercise, and more would be better.

NUTRITION FOR THE ADULT DOG

Adult German Shepherds need a bal-anced diet with high-quality protein to build and repair muscles, skin, organs, and blood. Dogs use the fat in their diet as a main source of ener-gy, so the quality and quantity of fat in their food is important. Too much fat can cause loose stools and also tax the digestive system, especially the pancreas, yet too little fat is not healthy either. Kibble diets are gener-ally high in carbohydrates from grains or potatoes. These carbohydrates can

regular exercise leads to weakened muscles, including the heart. Insufficient exercise can also make a dog restless and irritable, which can cause behavior problems like exces-sive barking, overprotectiveness, or repeated escape attempts.

For good conditioning exercise, nothing beats free-running play on soft ground with other dogs. This isn't always practical or possible though, so it's important to provide some other exercise that gives your German Shepherd a good aerobic

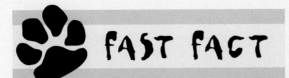

FAST FACT

A dog of the proper weight will have a well-defined waistline that's easily noticeable when looking down at his back from above.

be used by the dog for energy but are not generally as digestible for that purpose as fats.

Most people feed their dogs commercial dry and canned foods. These vary in the quality of their ingredients, which is usually reflected in the price of the products. Buying rock bottom–priced dog food is usually no bargain, because you can be fairly certain that cheap food contains cheap ingredients. Though a dog can survive on food made with low-quality protein and excessive carbohydrates, he will not thrive on that diet. An expensive price tag does not guarantee excellence, though, so always read the ingredient list carefully.

More and more dog owners are starting to include fresh meat, bones, and vegetables in their dogs' diets. If you're interested in feeding your dog fresh foods, be sure to read up on proper nutrition for shepherds, so you'll know how to provide your dog with a well-balanced diet. There are a number of books with healthy homemade diets for dogs and several good Internet chat groups for dog owners who choose to feed their shepherds fresh raw or home-cooked foods.

A healthy diet must be readily digestible, nutritionally balanced, and fed in the correct amount for the individual dog. Dogs gain weight if they consume more food than they use for exercise and body maintenance. They lose weight if they burn more calories than they get from the food they're eating. This seems so simple, but many dog owners don't realize the importance of observing their dog's weight and adjusting his food intake accordingly. Few responsible dog owners would underfeed their dogs to

Between meals, your shepherd will enjoy treats he can chew, like this rawhide bone.

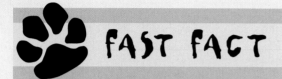

unhealthy thinness, but many over-feed them to a state of morbid obesity. Extra pounds on a dog steal years from his life span, so don't let your shepherd become obese.

It's easy to determine if your dog is maintaining a healthy weight. Stand him up and look down at his back from above. You should be able to see a waist between your dog's last set of ribs and his hips. If there's little to no waistline, the dog is overweight. If you can see hip and spine bones clearly outlined through the fur, your dog is too thin.

Now look at your standing dog from the side. There should be a bit of a tuck-up to the lower abdomen, just ahead of the rear legs. If there's little to no tuck-up, the dog is overweight. If you can see the curve of every rib through the fur, the dog is too thin.

Now feel your dog's side with the tips of your fingers. You should be able to count his ribs without having to dig for them. If you can feel each rib with your fingertips, he's lean

enough. Then run your flat palm along your dog's side. If it feels firm and smooth, then he has enough flesh and muscle. If you feel every rib against your hand, the dog is too thin.

When it comes to health, a lean body in a dog is generally preferable to a fat one. Numerous scientifically controlled experiments have proven that lean animals (including humans) tend to have fewer chronic health problems and tend to have a longer life span than normal weight or slightly overweight individuals of the same species.

JOBS FOR YOUR SHEPHERD

German Shepherds have proven their worth over and over again in the assistance dog work world. Shepherds make reliable service dogs, helping people with physical or emotional disabilities do things they could not do without help. A well-trained service dog can do most of the tasks that would otherwise force a person to hire a human helper. The dogs carry groceries, retrieve dropped or distant items, pull wheelchairs, help the person in and out of bed, help the person dress and undress, fetch drinks from the fridge, open and close heavy doors, help with laundry, make beds, and perform many other helpful tasks.

German Shepherds have long served as guide dogs to the blind. The first guide dog in the United States was a female German Shepherd named Buddy. Buddy and all the dogs who have followed in her paw prints safely lead blind individuals through major cities, sprawled-out towns, and rural farms. A guide dog learns to recognize and avoid situations that might endanger his blind partner. Normally, when the person

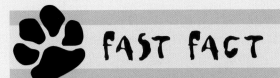

FAST FACT

Dogs gain weight when they consume more food than they burn through exercise and body maintenance.

commands the dog to move forward, that's what the dog will immediately do. However, if the dog is commanded to do anything that would endanger his partner, he will refuse to move.

German Shepherds can also serve as hearing assistance dogs. These dogs are trained to alert their deaf or hearing-impaired human partner to important sounds, like the person's name, a baby's cry, the alarm clock's ring, the oven timer's buzz, and the fire alarm's wail. When he hears the sound, the dog is trained to go to the person and give her a signal, such as a nudge of his nose against her hand, which indicates that he has heard something she needs to know about. Once the hearing dog has the person's attention, he will indicate the source of the sound, so she can respond to it appropriately.

THERAPY DOGS

Because they are so intelligent and strong, German Shepherds are popular service dogs.

Even though shepherds don't typically seek attention from strangers, they seem to know just how to comfort victims of traumatic events. Many shepherds participate in pet-assisted therapy, visiting nursing homes and other care facilities, bringing residents the joy and unconditional affection only a dog can give.

Some German Shepherds serve as emotional-therapy dogs, helping patients open up to something outside themselves and begin to heal. Even victims of trauma, who lose the ability to talk or relate to other human beings, often find great comfort and safety in the nonjudgmental affection of a large, gentle German Shepherd.

SEARCH-AND-RESCUE (SAR) DOGS

A search-and-rescue dog is trained to do what comes naturally—follow his nose—and his nose can lead his handler to just about anything with the person's scent he has been asked to seek. The SAR dog can find items the size of a match that the person had handled and dropped weeks earlier in the middle of a hundred-acre field. Something like this is not even particularly difficult for a trained dog to find. The scenting capability of a SAR-trained German Shepherd is phenomenal.

SAR dogs must not be aggressive toward people or other

Pet-assisted therapy helps patients open up emotionally and speeds up the healing process.

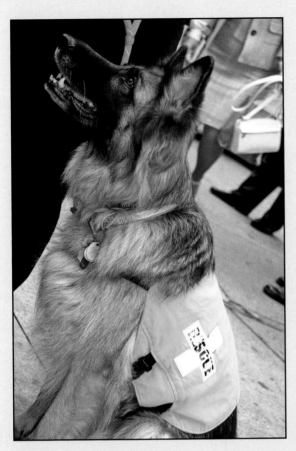

Search-and-rescue dogs undergo special training that allows them to track people by their scent and helps them respond in disaster situations.

dogs, because they often need to work in a group search setting. They must be able to ignore exciting fresh deer and rabbit trails that cross the faint scent of the lost person they are following. They must be courageous enough to ride in open boats, helicopters, snowplows, ski lifts, and any other conveyance that can take SAR teams to where the missing person may have left her scent.

SAR work requires the dogs and their handlers to be strong, fit, and able to work long hours with little rest, night or day, in freezing storms, or desert heat. The only pay the handlers receive is the satisfaction of having helped rescue a person in trouble, and German Shepherds are also satisfied with that kind of pay.

CANINE GOOD CITIZEN (CGC)

The AKC's Canine Good Citizen (CGC) test is open to dogs of all breeds and mixes. This test involves 10 exercises that assess the dog's social and obedience skills. He must walk on a leash without pulling; sit; lie down; walk through a crowd; ignore a dog that is close by; stay where told; come when called; let strangers pet him, groom him, and hold him while his owner leaves the room for several minutes; withstand sudden loud noises or visual stimulation; and demonstrate a few other real-life skills.

Dogs that pass the CGC test are issued certificates celebrating that achievement. The benefits of that certification go beyond the obvious one of having a well-behaved dog. Some homeowners' insurance companies require CGC certification before they insure owners of certain breeds. Some communities are considering lower license fees for dogs that have earned CGC certificates, and some landlords will reduce, or even waive, their standard pet deposit for CGC dogs.

TEMPERAMENT TESTING

The German Shepherd Dog Club of America sponsors Temperament Evaluation tests, held by local and regional German Shepherd clubs around the United States. At these events, a trained evaluator observes each dog in turn as they go through a series of structured exercises. Any breed can take the test, but it was originally designed for testing German Shepherd temperament.

The exercises present specific situations, such as a friendly stranger, a threatening stranger, the startling opening of an umbrella, the sound of gunfire, and more. The evaluator scores the dog on courage, protectiveness, and other qualities of temperament.

A dog that passes all parts of the Temperament test with high marks possesses the proper temperament for a working German Shepherd. Those that pass receive a certificate and are permitted to add the initials "TT" (Temperament Tested) after their name, to signify this achievement.

ADVANCED TRAINING

If you like teaching your pup the basics, you'll probably enjoy teaching him advanced skills even more. These are the skills needed for show dogs.

CONFORMATION: Conformation shows are competitive events where German Shepherds and purebred dogs of other breeds are judged against the written Standard of Perfection for their breed. The Standard describes the ideal appearance, gait, and temperament of the breed. Males and females are judged separately, and the winner in each sex is awarded from one to five championship points. The number of points is determined by how many dogs compete. Winners in both sexes are then judged together, along with champions, and one dog among them is selected as the Best of Breed (BOB) for that day. That dog then goes on to compete against the other BOB winners in his group. German Shepherds are in the Herding Group. The winner from each of the seven groups (Sporting, Hound, Working, Terrier, Toy, Non-Sporting, and Herding) then competes against the other group winners for Best in Show.

A Conformation dog must be kept in the peak of health in order to win. The dog's muscles should be well developed and firm, his eyes should be bright and clear, his coat

Training your German Shepherd to become a show dog requires a lot of hard work, but many owners find showing their dogs to be an extremely satisfying endeavor.

should shine. Conformation dogs are trained to trot so the judge can see how they move ("gait") and pose for presentation and examination by the judge ("stack"). German Shepherds are presented in a different stack than other breeds. Instead of posing with legs four-square or both hind legs stretched back, shepherds are posed with one rear leg under the body and the other extended back, This stack shows off the desired angulation of the German Shepherd's rear quarters.

A Conformation show dog must allow himself to be handled all over by the judge, including mouth, teeth, and, for males, testicles. In the conformation ring, the judge evaluates both temperament and physique for conformance to the Breed Standard.

OBEDIENCE: Obedience Trials are frequently held in conjunction with Conformation shows, though sometimes Obedience trials are stand-alone events. Obedience tests a dog's response to his handler. The dog

THE COSTS OF COMPETITION

If you decide to get involved in competition sports with your German Shepherd, the annual cost of your dog will skyrocket, as you add on the following expenses:

Entry fees: $20 to $30 for each class entered. Depending on which sports and how many you compete in with your dog, entry fees for one show or trial can run from $20 to $100, or more.

Transportation: Fuel for your car or motor home to drive to shows within driving distance, and plane fare for important shows farther from home, such as the German Shepherd Dog Club of America's annual National Specialty show.

Lodging: Hotel or motel rooms range from $80 to several hundred dollars a night, depending on quality, location, and whether or not the pet fee charged by the hotel is refundable. At some events, participants are permitted to camp on the show grounds. If you own a motor home or camping trailer, this option usually costs from $15 to $50 a night.

Meals away from home: Budget appropriately, depending on your appetite and tastes.

Handler's fees: $100 to $600 or more per show. Hiring a professional handler to exhibit your German Shepherd in Conformation, instead of handling him yourself, can increase your dog's success in the show ring, but the cost of earning those awards will increase as well.

Photographs of wins: When your shepherd wins at a show, captures a title, or earns a perfect score, you will want to get a photograph to remember the day. Sponsoring clubs arrange to have one or more professional photographers on site at the show to provide that service to exhibitors. Dog show photographers generally charge between $25 and $35 per print.

must obey verbal commands and hand signals immediately, precisely, and willingly. The handler is allowed to command the dog once, and then must give no further cues until the exercise is finished. Between exercises the handler is allowed to praise and pet the dog, but the dog must remain under the handler's control.

There are several levels of difficulty in Obedience, with a title to be earned at each level by attaining three to ten qualifying scores at that level. A qualifying score in

Obedience is 170 or better. A perfect score is 200.

Novice Obedience requires the dog to heel close to his handler's left side, both on and off leash, as they walk, turn, halt, and change speeds as directed by the judge. The dog must stay when told, then come when called and sit facing the handler within easy reach. Each dog must do an individual stand-stay, allowing the judge to touch him, and then they all perform sit- and down-stays together, for one and three minutes, respectively. Three qualifying scores at the Novice level earn a dog the CD (Companion Dog) title.

The next level is Open, where the dogs follow a pattern off leash as the judge directs. There are jumps and retrieving exercises in Open; for the group sit- and down-stays, the handlers must leave their dogs and wait out of sight for three and five minutes, respectively. Three qualifying scores in Open earn the title CDX (Companion Dog Excellent).

The next level in Obedience is called Utility. Here the dog does a silent signal exercise. The handler cues the dog to sit, down, stand, stay, and come, using only hand signals. For a send-out, the dog must run to the far end of the ring, turn, and sit facing the handler, waiting to be signaled which of two jumps he must leap on the way back in. For a directed retrieve, the judge designates which of three cotton work gloves the handler will send the dog to fetch.

There is also a scent discrimination exercise in Utility. This requires matching sets of five metal articles and five leather articles. These can be dumbbell-shaped articles manufactured for Obedience training, or common metal or leather objects in sets of five identical items (for example, five identical leather moccasins and five identical metal tablespoons). The objects are placed on the floor at the other end of the ring, after the handler holds one for a few moments to scent it. On the judge's signal, the handler sends the dog to find the scented item. The dog sniffs the pile of identical articles and retrieves the correct one, or so the handler hopes. An item of the other material is then scented by the handler and placed among the other identical articles, and the dog must find it by scent and carry it to the handler.

Three qualifying scores in Utility earn the UD (Utility Dog) title.

Dogs can also earn the UDX (Utility Dog Excellent) title by getting qualifying scores in both Open and Utility classes at the same trial, and doing that ten times.

RALLY: In Rally, the dog and handler heel together around a course of numbered stations, each with a sign indicating an exercise for the handler and dog to perform. About fifty exercises test the dog and handler's teamwork skills. In Rally the handler is permitted to talk to and encourage the dog as much as she wants. The handler is allowed to praise the dog, but not pet him, both while performing the exercises and when moving between them.

Novice level Rally is performed on leash. Advanced and Excellent Rally levels are performed off leash. A perfect score in AKC Rally is 100. Titles are earned at each level with three qualifying scores of 70 or higher. The titles are Rally Novice (RN), Rally Advanced (RA), and Rally Excellent (RE). Another title, the Rally Advanced Excellent (RAE), can be earned after completing the RE. This additional title requires the team to earn qualifying scores in both Advanced and Excellent classes at the same trial, and do that ten times.

Some Rally exercises are similar to Obedience exercises—sits, downs, stays, call-fronts, finishes-to-heel, stands, and figure-8s. There are also challenging exercises not used in Obedience, with heeling through serpentines and elongated spirals among them. Rally calls for many different turns, with not only 90° and 180° turns, as encountered in Obedience, but also 270° and 360° turns to both left and right.

In Rally, the judge only tells the team when to start. From then on, the handler guides herself and her dog around the ring, following the course without direction from the judge. The team moves from sign to sign in numbered order, performing each exercise as described in the regulations.

Gentleness on the part of the handler and willingness on the part of the dog are hallmarks of a well-tuned Rally team. Everything a dog and handler do is score-able from the moment they enter the Rally ring gate until they leave the ring after their run. Handler mistakes—such as guiding the dog with a tight leash, making collar-jerk corrections, or speaking sharply to the dog—or dog mistakes, like being uncooperative in getting into start position, can lose points for the team before they even start the course.

When the handler and dog are at the start sign, the judge asks, "Are you ready?" The handler checks her dog to be sure he's in position beside her, and then replies to the judge, "Yes," or "Ready." The judge then says, "Forward," and, from that point on, says nothing more. The judge silently follows behind or to the side of the team at a distance and angle that provides the best view of each station. The judge scores the team's performance as they proceed from sign to sign, doing each exercise along the course.

The handler may speak to and encourage the dog as much as she wants. Repeated cues and signals are not penalized, and if the team cannot successfully perform an exercise on their first attempt, a retry is allowed. The retry costs the team three points off their final score, but, if the retry is successful, that three-point deduction is less "expensive" than losing a full ten points for incorrectly performing the station.

AGILITY: For Agility, dogs are judged on speed and accuracy over a course of jumps, tunnels, ramps, and other obstacles. Each dog is timed as

Jumps in an Agility competition range from four inches to two feet or more.

A shepherd participates in the broad jump, another obstacle in the Agility competition.

he individually races over a numbered obstacle course, as directed by his handler. In Agility, the dog performs the jumps and obstacles and the handler does not. The handler may run with the dog, directing him from up close, from behind, or from the side at a greater distance from the dog.

The experienced Agility dog learns to respond instantly to subtle movements of his handler's shoulders, hips, and knees on the course, as cues for changes in direction or pace. Most handlers also use hand signals and verbal cues to give their dogs specific information, like which one of two side-by-side obstacles to tackle. Handlers may also talk, clap, praise, and verbally encourage the dog, but may not touch the dog or any of the obstacles.

In Agility, a dog can earn titles at the Novice, Open, and Excellent levels by earning three qualifying scores for each level. First- through fourth-place ribbons are awarded to the dogs with the fewest faults and the fastest run times. Dogs compete for placements only against other dogs of their same approximate height. A dog can earn titles without placing.

To determine the proper jump height division for the dog, a judge at an Agility trial will measure him at the withers (the highest point of the shoulder) and issue a height card with the dog's official measurement.

Jumps are adjusted from four inches (10 cm) high to 24 inches (61 cm) or more. All the jumps on a course are set at the same height. Tall dogs have higher jumps than short dogs, which helps make Agility fair for all. The average German Shepherd height ranges from 22 to 26 inches (56 to 66 cm) tall, so they will jump 16, 20, or 24 inches (41, 51, or 61 cm) in American Kennel Club Agility. Only the jumps are adjusted for the dogs' heights; all other obstacles are the same for all dogs.

AKC Agility trials include Standard Agility, a course that uses all the obstacles, and Jumpers with Weaves, a course of only jumps and weave poles. There is now also a challenging course, the FAST class, where the handler, from a distance, directs the dog over part of the course. Other organizations offer games similar to AKC's and some that are very different.

CHAPTER EIGHT

Caring for Your Senior Dog

German Shepherds become seniors at around 10 or 12 years of age. As your shepherd ages, his body will go through gradual changes, both externally and internally. Dogs experience many of the same age-related health issues that people do. The digestive system slows down and becomes less efficient; metabolism may slow, too. The heart gradually weakens, as do other muscles. Tumors, cysts, and other growths may appear. Hearing and eyesight start to fail. Cancer, heart disease, diabetes, stroke, and nerve disorders—all these health problems can plague senior dogs just as they do senior humans.

Incontinence of bladder and bowels is a problem that occurs with

Going a little gray and having less energy as they age is natural for German Shepherds.

many dogs in their senior years. Medication can alleviate some cases of incontinence, but not all. It's important to help your elderly shepherd maintain his dignity, and incontinence can make that challenging. Most incontinent senior dogs are aware that they are soiling themselves and your floors. Your shepherd may feel frustrated and ashamed, so try to disguise your own annoyance with the mess and treat your dog with as much respect as possible.

Do your best to keep the incontinent dog clean, so his skin isn't scalded by urine. You will need to change his bedding every time he soils it. One way to cut down on laundry is to keep a doggie diaper on your incontinent shepherd. This must be changed numerous times a day, but that's still less work than multiple loads of laundry, and probably less humiliating for the dog than peeing on his own bed.

There are no cures for aging, but there are ways to make your shepherd's senior years more comfortable and pleasant.

NUTRITION

As a dog ages, his digestive system often becomes less efficient, making it more important than ever for the

To keep your shepherd from putting on extra weight in his senior years, be sure to reduce his caloric intake to match his activity level. Too much food and not enough exercise can make your shepherd overweight.

proteins and fats he consumes to be high quality and easily digested. Most senior dogs exercise less than they did when they were younger, so you often have to reduce the senior dog's calorie intake to prevent weight gain.

An elderly dog in good health can maintain proper weight on the same food he's always eaten, but the serving size must be reduced to match his lower metabolism and activity level.

Some senior dogs develop digestion or metabolism problems. For these dogs it may not be enough to simply reduce the size of their meals. They might need a different diet than the one that sustained them when they were younger. Ask your veterinarian to help you find the best way to keep your senior dog's weight under control.

If your senior shepherd has heart, liver, or kidney problems, he may also need a special diet. Prescription diets, available from veterinarians, are formulated specifically to help the dog stay as healthy as possible, despite impaired organ function.

EXERCISE

Your senior shepherd still needs regular daily exercise to keep his heart, lungs, and muscles healthy and working properly. Lack of exercise will cause muscles, including the heart

muscle, to weaken and deteriorate. This will predispose an inactive dog to become overweight. The combination of muscle atrophy and weight gain leads to even more inactivity, in a downward spiral of weakness and worsening health.

You can avoid this unhealthy deterioration by keeping your shep-

The level of exercise a young German Shepherd enjoys may be too much for him in his senior years.

herd active as he ages. Obviously, this does not mean you should take your elderly shepherd mountain climbing or swimming in whitewater rapids. It is not safe to ask a senior dog to keep up that level of activity, even if he did it easily when he was younger. Few senior humans can safely revisit the extreme activities of their youth, and neither can dogs. However, if you continue giving your senior dog moderate daily exercise that keeps his heart, lungs, and muscles in good condition as he ages, he will stay healthy and active years longer than an out-of-condition dog.

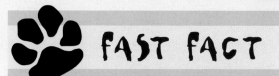

FAST FACT

When a dog loses his hearing or vision, he may still function quite well, as his other senses compensate somewhat for the loss.

Make a point of giving your elder shepherd a daily walk or play a few rounds of fetch with him, but never exercise him to the point of exhaustion. As he ages, be willing to allow those walks to become slower. Let him take some time to smell the bunnies.

OLD AGE AND SAYING GOOD-BYE

Eventually the time will come for you and your beloved elderly German Shepherd to say good-bye to each other. This is a sad time, but bittersweet as well, because your memories encompass all the good times and some of the rough spots you two have traveled together. Your dog is not alone in his aging—you have aged too, though his dog years have run out before your human years.

Your shepherd may begin to slow down toward the end of his life, yet he's still the same friend he has always been. Take time out and remember to spend time with him in his golden years.

Photographs of you with your dog can help soothe the pain in the difficult time that follows your shepherd's passing.

When you know your shepherd's time is getting close, there are some things you can do to ease this final transition for you both.

Take some new photographs of your shepherd. If possible, visit a few of the places that hold good memories for the two of you, and have a friend photograph you and your dog together there.

Write down your feelings in a journal. Jot down disjointed thoughts or form your words into poetry. Either way, it will help you release some of the outsize emotions you are probably feeling.

Pick a special spot to bury your dog's final remains or scatter his ashes after he passes. Take your dog there, if possible, and share a picnic, so the spot holds a recent memory of a happy time together.

Have a party for your dog and invite the people who care deeply

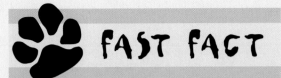

FAST FACT

After your pet passes away, you'll have to make final arrangements. The most common methods of laying a pet to rest are cremation and full body burial. Most veterinarians offer cremation services and pet cemetery recommendations. If your vet doesn't, you can locate a private crematorium or pet cemetery through the Web site of the International Association of Pet Cemeteries and Crematories, www.iaopc.com.

for both of you. They deserve an opportunity to say good-bye, too. Let people share their memories and feelings about your shepherd. Tape-

record or videotape that sharing time—it may be very healing for you to listen to or watch the tape in six months or a year.

Your dog may pass away in his sleep, or he may cling stubbornly to this world. As our dogs' best friends and lifelong caregivers, we have the option to provide the final kindness to our dogs of a painless passing. If your shepherd is suffering in his last days, talk over that final option with your veterinarian and decide if that is the right course to take.

When you and your shepherd say your final good-bye for this lifetime, comfort yourself by knowing that you've loved your old friend in life—and in death—as best you could.

Organizations to Contact

American Animal Hospital Association
12575 West Bayaud Ave.
Lakewood, CO 80228
Phone: 303-986-2800
Fax: 800-252-2242
Email: info@aahanet.org
Web site: www.aahanet.org

American German Shepherd Rescue Association, Inc.
P.O. Box 1445
Gridley, CA 95948
Phone: 707-994-5241
Email: lindakury@saber.net
Web site: www.agsra.com

American Kennel Club
260 Madison Ave
New York, NY 10016
Phone: 212-696-8200
Web site: www.akc.org

Association of Pet Dog Trainers
150 Executive Center Drive, Box 35
Greenville, SC 29615
Phone: 1-800-738-3647
Fax: 1-864-331-0767
Email: information@apdt.com
Web site: www.apdt.com

The British Association for German Shepherd Dogs
81 Park View Road
Sutton Coalfield
West Midlands B74 4PS
United Kingdom
Phone: 0121-353-9872
Email: bagsd@freeuk.com
Web site: www.bagsd.net

The Canadian Kennel Club
89 Skyway Avenue, Suite 100
Etobicoke, Ontario
M9W 6R4
Canada
Phone: 416-675-5511
Fax: 416-675-6506
Email: information@ckc.ca
Web site: www.ckc.ca/en/

Canine Eye Registration Foundation
1717 Philo Road
P.O. Box 3007
Urbana, IL 61803-3007
Phone: 217-693-4800
Fax: 217-693-4801
Email: cerf@vmdb.org
Web site: www.vmdb.org/cerf.html

Delta Society
875 124th Avenue NE, Suite 101
Bellevue, WA 98005
Phone: 425-226-7357
Fax: 425-679-5539
Email: info@deltasociety.org
Web site: www.deltasociety.org

**German Shepherd Dog Club
of America**
Sharon Allbright,
corresponding secretary
P.O. Box 429
Applegate, CA 95703
Phone: 530-878-8803
Fax: 530-878-2826
Email: sharlen@foothill.net
Web site: www.gsdca.org/

**German Shepherd Schutzhund
Club of Canada**
139 Hawkmere Road
Chestermere, Alberta
T1K 1T5
Canada
Phone: 403-273-5580
Fax: 403-204-3348
Web site: www.gsscc.ca

**The Kennel Club
of the United Kingdom**
1-5 Clarges Street
Piccadilly
London W1J 8AB
United Kingdom
Phone: 0870 606 6750

Fax: 020 7518 1058
Web site: www.thekennelclub.org.uk

**National Association of Dog
Obedience Instructors**
PMB 369
729 Grapevine Hwy
Hurst, TX 76054-2085
Email: corrsec2@nadoi.org
Web site: www.nadoi.org

**National Association of
Professional Pet Sitters**
17000 Commerce Parkway, Suite C
Mt. Laurel, NJ 08054
Phone: 856-439-0324
Fax: 856-439-0525
Email: napps@ahint.com
Web site: www.petsitters.org

National Dog Registry
P.O. Box 51105
Mesa, AZ 85208
Phone: 800-NDR-DOGS
Email: info@nationaldogregistry.com
Web site:
www.nationaldogregistry.com

**North American Dog Agility
Council (NADAC)**
11522 South Highway 3
Cataldo, ID 83810
Email: info@nadac.com
Web site: www.nadac.com

North American Flyball Association (NAFA)
1400 West Devon Avenue, #512
Chicago, IL 60660
Phone: 800-318-6312
Fax: same as phone
Email: flyball@flyball.org
Web site: www.flyball.org

Orthopedic Foundation for Animals (OFA)
2300 East Nifong Boulevard
Columbia, MO 65201-3806
Phone: 573-442-0418
Fax: 573-875-5073
Email: ofa@offa.org
Web site: www.offa.org

Pet Sitters International
418 East King Street
King, NC 27021-9163
Phone: 336-983-9222
Fax: 336-983-3755
Web site: www.petsit.com

Therapy Dogs International, Inc.
88 Bartley Road
Flanders, NJ 07836
Phone: 973-252-9800
Fax: 973-252-7171
Email: tdi@gti.net
Web site: www.tdi-dog.org

UK National Pet Register
74 North Albert Street, Dept 2
Fleetwood, Lancashire
FY7 6BJ
United Kingdom
Web site:
www.nationalpetregister.org

United States Dog Agility Association, Inc. (USDAA)
P.O. Box 850955
Richardson, TX 75085-0955
Phone: 972-487-2200
Fax: 972-272-4404
Email: info@usdaa.com
Web site: www.usdaa.com

World Canine Freestyle Organization (WCFO)
P.O. Box 350122
Brooklyn, NY 11235-2525
Phone: 718-332-8336
Fax: 718-646-2686
Email: wcfodogs@aol.com
Web site:
www.worldcaninefreestyle.org

Further Reading

Aloff, Brenda. *Canine Body Language, a Photographic Guide*. Wenatchee, Wash.: Dogwise Publishing, 2005.

Barwig, Susan. *German Shepherd Book*. Wheat Ridge, Colo.: Hoflin, 1987.

Carlson, James, and Lisa Giffin. *Dog Owner's Home Veterinary Handbook*. 3rd ed. New York: Howell Book House, 1999.

Dennison, Pamela. *Click Your Way to Rally Obedience*. Loveland, Colo.: Alpine Publishing, 2006.

Green, Peter, and Mario Migliorini. *New Secrets of Show Dog Handling*. Loveland, Colo.: Alpine Publishing, 2002.

Handler, Barbara. *Successful Obedience Handling*. 2nd ed. Loveland, Colo.: Alpine Publishing, 2003.

Hoffman, Gary. *Hiking With Your Dog*. 3rd ed. La Crescenta, Calif.: Mountain 'N Air Books, 2002.

Jones, Deb. *Click Here for a Well-Trained Dog*. Franklin, NY: Howln Moon, 2002.

Koshar, Claire. *A Guide to Dog Sports*. Wilsonville, Ore.: Doral Publishing, 2002.

Lanting, Fred. *Total German Shepherd Dog*. 2nd ed. Wheat Ridge, Colo.: Hoflin Publishing, 1999.

O'Neil, Jacqueline. *All About Agility*. New York: Howell Book House, 1998.

Pitcairn, Richard, and Susan Pitcairn. *Dr. Pitcairn's Complete Guide To Natural Health For Dogs & Cats*. 3rd ed. Emmaus, Pa.: Rodale, 2005.

Shojai, Amy. *First Aid Companion for Dogs & Cats*. Emmaus, Pa.: Rodale, 2001.

Strickland, Winifred. *Expert Obedience Training for Dogs*. 4th ed. New York: Howell Book House, 2003.

Internet Resources

www.agsra.com

The Web site of the American German Shepherd Rescue Association includes an annually updated directory of German Shepherd rescue groups and organizations.

www.aspca.org/apcc

The ASPCA Animal Poison Control Center provides lifesaving information for pet owners. The center also has a hot line available for emergencies: 888-426-4435

www.avma.org

The American Veterinary Medical Association Web site provides a wealth of information on canine health and welfare issues for pet owners.

http://clickertraining.com

Karen Pryor Clicker Training is an educational resource with information and how-to tips about the modern, non-force way of educating dogs through clicker training, a form of operant conditioning that is both effective and enjoyable.

www.healthypet.com

The Web site of the American Animal Hospital Association has lists of accredited veterinary hospitals in every state, along with up-to-date pet health info.

www.petfinder.com

A nationwide database of adoptable pets, which also provides listings of shelters and German Shepherd rescue groups.

www.petsitters.org

The Web site of the National Association of Professional Pet Sitters can be used to help German Shepherd owners locate a professional pet sitter in their area.

www.rintintin.com

The official written and photographic history of the famous movie star German Shepherd, Rin Tin Tin, and his equally famous progeny.

www.upei.ca/cidd/intro.htm

The Canine Inherited Disorders Database provides in-depth information on the hereditary disorders of dogs.

www.vdhaonline.org

The Web site of the Vietnam Dog Handlers Association includes photos and personal accounts of German Shepherds in action during the Vietnam War.

Index

adoption, pet, 37–39
    See also ownership
The Adventures of Rin Tin Tin (TV show), 22
Agility competition sport, 93–95
    See also dog shows
Alsatian Wolf Dog. *See* German Shepherds
American Animal Hospital Association
    (AAHA), 41
American German Shepherd Rescue
    Association (AGSRA), 38
American Kennel Club (AKC), 22–23, 30,
    87–88, 95
assistance dogs. *See* service dogs
Association for German Shepherds (Verein
    für Deutsche Schäferhunde), 19

barking, 32
bathing, 54–56
    See also grooming
behavior, 10, 50, 60–61
    See also training
bloat and torsion, 76–79
boarding kennels, 72
    See also traveling
breed history, 18–22
breed standards, 22–25
breeders, 36–37, 44
Breeder's Code, 36–37
Buddy (guide dog), 14, 85

cancer, 80–81
Canine Good Citizen (CGC) test, 87–88
coat, 12–13, 25
cognitive development, 50–51
color, 12–13, 23, 25
    See also physical characteristics
competition sports, 14, 92–95
    See also dog shows

Conformation dog shows, 13, 23, 36,
    40–41, 88–89
    See also dog shows
costs, 15–17
    dog show, 90
    See also insurance, pet

day care, doggie, 72
death, 99–101
degenerative myelopathy (DM), 79–80
dental care, 53–54
    See also health
diet. *See* nutrition
diseases, 47, 66, 79–81
DNA profiling, 30
dog shows, 88–91
    and competition sports, 14, 40–41,
        92–95
    Conformation, 13, 23, 36, 40–41, 88–89
    cost of, 90
    grooming, 57–58
Duncan, Lee, 21
dysplasia, 46–47, 66, 75–76

emotions, 13–14
exercise, 10, 15, 68–69, 81–82, 98–99
    See also health
exocrine pancreatic insufficiency (EPI), 63,
    80

feeding schedules, 49–50
    See also nutrition
first aid supplies, 58, 79
fleas, 63–64
food. *See* nutrition
Frank, Morris, 14

gait, 11–12, 25, 67, 89

Gastric-Dilatation Volvulus (GDV), 76–79
gender, 34–35
genetic defects, 62–63, 75–77, 79–80
    See also health
German Shepherd Dog Club of America
    (GSDCA), 19, 36–37, 88, 90
German Shepherds
    breed history, 18–22
    breed standards, 22–25
    choosing of, as pets, 34–41
    and cognitive development, 50–51
    colors, 12–13, 23, 25
    costs of care, 15–17
    emotions of, 13–14
    environment for, 14–15
    and exercise, 10, 15, 68–69, 81–82,
        98–99
    gait of, 11–12, 25, 67, 89
    genetic defects, 62–63, 75–77, 79–80
    grooming, 16–17, 52–58
    intelligence of, 13
    jobs for, 9–10, 14, 20, 84–87
    life expectancy, 96
    in movies, 20–22
    physical characteristics, 9, 11–14, 23–25
    popularity of, 22
    as service dogs, 14, 84–87
    size, 11, 23
    and socialization, 47, 50–52, 67–68
    temperament testing, 88
    training, 15, 16, 39, 58–61, 70–71, 88–95
    traveling with, 71–73
    in World Wars I and II, 19–20, 21
    See also dog shows; health; ownership
Germany, 18–20
grooming
    cost of, 16–17
    for dog shows, 57–58
    puppies, 52–57
guide dogs, 14, 85
    See also service dogs

health
    dental care, 53–54

diseases, 47, 66, 79–81
exercise, 10, 15, 68–69, 81–82, 98–99
genetic defects, 62–63, 75–77, 79–80
and nutrition, 15, 17, 48–49, 66–67, 70,
    82–84, 97–98
parasites, 63–65
and puppies, 45–47
and senior dogs, 96–99
and vaccinations, 44, 47–48, 65–66
and veterinary care, 16, 41–42, 46–48,
    74–75
heartworm, 64–65
hip dysplasia, 46–47, 66, 75–76
history, breed, 18–22
Horand v Grafeth (sheep dog), 19
household rules, 60–61
    See also training
housetraining, 58–60
    See also training
Humane Society of the United States, 30

identification, 27–30, 44
incontinence, 96–97
Indefinite Listing Privilege (ILP), 36
insurance, pet, 32–33
    See also costs
intelligence, 13
International Association of Pet
    Cemeteries and Crematories, 101

jobs (service dogs), 9–10, 14, 20, 84–87

legal issues, 26–27, 32, 33
    See also ownership
licensing, 27
life expectancy, 96

The Man from Hell's River (movie), 22
Meyer, Artur, 19
microchip implants, 27, 30
    See also identification
movies, 20–22

nail care, 56–58

See also grooming
Nannette (German Shepherd), 21
National Association of Professional Pet
    Sitters, 73
neutering, 30–32
nuisance laws, 32
    See also legal issues
nutrition, 15, 17, 66–67, 70, 82–84
    for puppies, 48–49
    and senior dogs, 97–98
    See also health

obedience
    training, 70–71
    trials, 89–91
Orthopedic Foundation for Animals, 76
ownership
    choosing the right dog, 34–39
    and death of your pet, 99–101
    and legal issues, 26–27, 32, 33
    responsibilities, 26–33
    and veterinary care, 41–42

pannus, 80
panosteitis, 63
parasites, 63–65
pedigree paper, 44
pet sitters, 72
    See also traveling
physical characteristics, 9, 11–14, 23–25
police service dogs, 14
popularity, 22
potty bell, 60
    See also housetraining
puppies, 39–41
    bathing, 54–56
    caring for, 43–50
    and dental care, 53–54
    grooming, 52–53
    nail care, 56–58
    and socialization, 47, 50–52
    training, 58–61
    See also German Shepherds
Puppy Kindergarten, 52

rally, 92–93
    See also dog shows
registration papers, 44
rescue organizations, 37–39
Rin Tin Tin (German Shepherd), 21–22

search-and-rescue (SAR) dogs, 86–87
    See also service dogs
senior dogs, 96–99
sense loss, 99
service dogs, 14, 35, 36, 84–87
shedding, 12–13, 52
The Silent Call (movie), 22
size, 11, 23
socialization, 47, 50–52, 67–68
spaying, 30–32
Standard of Perfection, 22–23, 88
Strongheart (German Shepherd), 20
supplies, 16–17
    first aid, 58, 79
    See also costs

tattoos, 27, 29–30
    See also identification
teeth, 24, 53–54
temperament testing, 88
theft, dog, 27
therapy dogs, 85–86
    See also service dogs
titles, 90–92, 94
    See also dog shows
toys. *See* supplies
training, 15, 39, 58–61
    advanced, 88–95
    cost of, 16
    obedience, 70–71
traveling, 71–73

utility trials, 91
    See also obedience

vaccinations, 44, 47–48, 65–66
    See also health
Verein für Deutsche Schäferhunde

(Association for German Shepherds),
19
veterinary care
    choosing, 41–42
    cost of, 16
    for puppies, 46–48
    regular check-ups, 74–75
    See also health

von Stephanitz, Max, 18–19
Von Willebrand's disease, 80

Warner Bros. Pictures, 21
    See also movies
World War I, 19–20, 21
World War II, 20

Contributors

SEPTEMBER MORN is a professional dog trainer and free-lance writer, whose articles have appeared in *Dog Fancy*, *Popular Dogs*, *Dogs For Kids*, *Dogs USA*, *Puppies USA*, *Clean Run*, and *Your Dog*. Her previous books include *Training Your Labrador Retriever* (Barron's, 2000) and *Housetraining* (2nd ed., Howell/Wiley, 2006). Her first purebred dog was a German Shepherd, whose pedigree included several of the Rin Tin Tin line. September owned and loved 10 more German Shepherds after that and competed in Obedience with them. September owns Dogs Love School, in Shelton, Washington, and currently shares her home and heart with three Rottweilers and two American Eskimo dogs.

Senior Consulting Editor **GARY KORSGAARD, DVM,** has had a long and distinguished career in veterinary medicine. After graduating from The Ohio State University's College of Veterinary Medicine in 1963, he spent two years as a captain in the Veterinary Corps of the U.S. Army. During that time he attended the Walter Reed Army Institute of Research and became Chief of the Veterinary Division for the Sixth Army Medical Laboratory at the Presidio, San Francisco.

In 1968 Dr. Korsgaard founded the Monte Vista Veterinary Hospital in Concord, California, where he practiced for 32 years as a small animal veterinarian. He is a past president of the Contra Costa Veterinary Association, and was one of the founding members of the Contra Costa Veterinary Emergency Clinic, serving as president and board member of that hospital for nearly 30 years.

Dr. Korsgaard retired in 2000, and currently enjoys golf, hiking, international travel, and spending time with his wife Susan and their three children and four grandchildren.